Practical Guide to

REIKI

an Ancient Healing Art

Practical Guide to

REIKI

an Ancient Healing Art

Klaudia Hochhuth

GEMCRAFT BOOKS

First published in 1993 by
Gemcraft Books
291-293 Wattletree Road East Malvern
Victoria 3145 Australia

Printed in Australia
by McPherson's Printing Group
on non-chlorine bleached paper
made from plantation pines.

National Library of Australia
Cataloguing-in-Publication data
    Hochhuth, Klaudia
     Practical guide to Reiki - an ancient healing art.

    Bibliography.
    ISBN 0 909223 57 2.

    1.Reiki (Healing system). I Title.

615.851

Dedication

This book is dedicated to my parents and my brother.

I'd like to extend my deepest gratitude to Susannah Brindle, Faith Brown, Eileen Chapman, Pavel Janousek, Melissa Jones, Mary-anne Rowe and Liz Widdop for supporting the work on my first Reiki book, and to Summerdot's Design for providing the Reiki clothes.

My special thanks go to Reiki Master Jim Frew - my 'Australian brother' and friend - for encouraging me to write this book and also for helping me 'to get rid of the German commas', a factor which people will understand if they have ever had to translate German into English! Through his practical and editorial advice and with his constant support I was able to fulfil this task. Together we had a lot of fun completing this project.

Author's Note

It is not an easy task to explain to someone exactly what Reiki is, either in writing or, for that matter, verbally. In fact, the task is about as difficult as describing the fragrance of an exotic flower which you have neither seen, nor heard of before.

So, just as it would be important to actually smell that flower to appreciate its fragrance, so it is equally important to experience a Reiki treatment to have any concept of this healing art and its possibilities.

However, there is also an intellectual component and a theoretical and historical background, and it is these aspects that I will endeavour to address in this book.

I trust that the book will fulfil this task, and will arouse in you a healthy curiosity. So, if this is your first encounter with this universal life force which we call Reiki, I hope that you will now seek a treatment, either from a practitioner, or maybe from a Reiki Master like myself.

Perhaps then you will understand why, in less than twenty-five years, the knowledge of this gentle healing art has spread from a single source on the island of Kauai in Hawaii, where for some thirty-five years Grand Master Hawayo Takata was the world's sole teacher of the Usui System of Natural Healing. Now there are many thousands of practitioners of the healing art worldwide, such has been its mass appeal.

We say that Reiki 'opens doors' and 'creates new paths'. I sincerely hope that, as a result of reading this book, you, dear reader, will be led to wonderful new opportunities, as happened to me almost ten years ago. To those who do choose this path, I wish you joy!

In conclusion, I would like to extend an open invitation to readers to write to me with their questions, thoughts and experiences. In this way the knowledge of Reiki can be continually shared for the benefit of everyone.

Klaudia Hochhuth, 1993

Contents

Appendix:

Part One

Reiki History and Theory

Chapter 1

What is Reiki ?

Reiki is a Japanese word representing Universal Life Energy. The syllable *Rei* describes the universal boundless aspect of this energy; whilst the syllable *ki* stands for 'life energy'. *Rei-ki* therefore means universal life energy or universal life force. It is infinite, and flows without ending. It is the energy of the entire cosmos - the vital life force that maintains all living things - the human beings, animals and plants that inhabit our planet.

You may have heard about Tai Chi, Aikido or Shiatsu. The syllables *ki* or *chi* likewise mean energy, as in Reiki. In other cultures you may refer to Light (Christianity) or Bio-plasmic Energy (Russian researchers) or Prana (Hinduism and Buddhism).

Reiki is a natural healing art, which was rediscovered in the mid-nineteenth century by a Christian educator named Dr. Mikao Usui. It is therefore called the Usui System of Natural Healing.

A practical and simple way of describing Reiki is channelling universal life energy through the laying on of hands.

Reiki, when activated and applied for purposes of healing, addresses body, mind and spirit. It accelerates the body's ability to heal physical ailments, and opens the mind and spirit to the underlying reasons of disease and pain, discomfort and blockages, which might have caused the problem in the first place. To find the reason behind the problem is the necessity for taking responsibility for your life and the joy and happiness of balanced wellness.

Reiki is a tool which can facilitate the discovery of your

spiritual path. Maybe you lost track of your spirituality a few months ago, perhaps a few years ago or even a very long time ago during your childhood, or maybe this is a path you have not yet found. Reiki is a gentle, but powerful way to access your spirituality and your purpose in life. It restores or creates that feeling of being at one with yourself, with humankind and our planet earth. It makes you feel 'at home'.

Reiki

Reiki is heaven shared through the hands,
Reiki is love teaching our hearts to expand,
Reiki is accepting our beautiful selves,
And finally believing in the simplicity that is life.

written by Sue Duff - 17.7.1991

Chapter 2

The History of Reiki
(as retold by Susannah Brindle)

A humble Christian professor was challenged in the pulpit by his valedictory students as to the literal truth of the healing miracles Jesus was said to have performed:

"If you really believe what Jesus said about his followers healing the sick, why aren't you doing it - and why should we students change our ways for such an unverified belief?"

It was Japan in the late 1800's. Dr. Mikao Usui's long search for the knowledge of the Christian ministry of healing - a search that can be called 'the story of Reiki' - began that day. He resigned his post as head of Doshisha University, Kyoto, and set sail for what he believed to be the heartland of pure Christianity - the United States of America. He soon discovered that Western Christianity was as ignorant of this ancient healing ability as he. Having learned that Buddha and his followers had healed in ways similar to Jesus, Dr. Usui pursued his search into the realms of Buddhism. After seven years he returned to Kyoto to deepen his search, visiting many Buddhist seats of learning and mastering first Chinese and then Sanskrit in order to have access to Buddhist texts of an increasing antiquity. After many years his perseverance was rewarded. In the library of a Zen monastery he discovered ancient symbols which he knew intuitively were what he had been seeking.

But how was he to apply them? In discussion with his friend, the Zen abbot, Dr. Usui realised he must now relinquish all human striving and simply await enlightenment. He chose to ascend the steep slopes of a holy mountain nearby, there to fast and meditate for twenty-one days. Such was the intensity of his search that Dr. Usui had confided to the abbot that without the enlightenment he sought he would not return alive.

So Dr. Usui sat down by clear running water and, building himself a little computation cairn of 21 stones, prepared to watch and wait.

In the pitch dark of pre-dawn there was but one stone left as Dr. Usui prepared to greet the light of the last day of his retreat and, perhaps, of his life. What followed was utterly unexpected, for only the mindfulness of his long and arduous search and the importance of his ultimate goal kept the pilgrim from dodging the hurtling bolt of Light which appeared from nowhere and struck him in the centre of his forehead.

How can one adequately describe the moment of enlightenment by Grace? (Enlightenment by grace is another meaning of the Japanese symbol for Reiki.) In an experience of pure colour representing every rainbow hue, then pure white light, and then gold, Dr Usui was shown the essence, the inner purpose, of each of the ancient symbols he had discovered in the Buddhist texts. He was flooded with a sense of total, committed acceptance.

Miraculously revitalised, he set off for Kyoto. On the homeward journey he discovered proof of the healing which now radiated from his hands: first he healed his own foot (injured in his haste to be on his way) and next, the toothache of an innkeeper's daughter. The old abbot received him, wrapped in layers of quilts to keep the cold from his bones. As Dr. Usui shared his wonderful adventures with his friend, he discovered that the healing energy was undeterred by distance. While speaking, Dr. Usui laid his hands upon the quilts and by the end of the story the abbot reported that he was no longer troubled with arthritic pain. They decided there could be no name other than Reiki which could be applied to this amazing energy.

With the encouragement of the Zen monks, Dr. Usui sought to deepen his understanding of this healing energy through first-hand experience. Feeling a concern to release people from lives of dishonesty, disease and misery, he left the monastery to go and live in the same conditions as those he sought to heal and rehabilitate. He became a familiar figure in one of Kyoto's worst slum areas, healing many and discovering a great deal about the emotional causes of disease.

A painful moment of reckoning came one evening seven years after Dr. Usui had begun his work in the slums. Through a chance meeting with a young man he had healed some years before, he discovered that many of his former patients had really not been ready to receive the healing offered. Unprepared for the responsibilities of contributing to life and to their fellow human beings, they had chosen to return to their ways of dishonesty, violence and disease.

The despair Dr. Usui felt at having 'wasted' seven years was profound. He blamed himself for failing to stress the importance of the spiritual aspects of healing and vowed that in future he would teach Reiki within the ethical principles of gentleness, trust, gratitude, honesty, and respect. He also vowed that never again would Reiki be given to those who did not show they valued this healing power.

Leaving Kyoto behind him, Dr. Usui began a long journey from the south to the north of the island of Hokkaido, visiting the busiest parts of each market town. His practice was to carry a blazing torch aloft (in spite of the daylight) and, when questioned as to his eccentric behaviour, he would reply that he was searching for those who needed Light in their sad, depressed lives, and that to those who really wanted the Light he would teach true healing of mind and body.

In one of these towns, he attracted the following of a forty-seven-year-old retired naval officer, Dr. Chujiro Hayashi. Dr. Hayashi joined Dr. Usui on his travels and the old Master ultimately named Dr. Hayashi as his successor in what came to be known as the Usui System of Natural Healing.

For the next fifteen years, Dr. Hayashi brought a quiet professionalism to the story of Reiki. Meticulous records of the many Reiki healings performed were kept at Dr. Hayashi's large clinic which serviced the huge Tokyo population. His was a flourishing practice attracting the well-educated and affluent in Tokyo society. On the surface it seemed as if Dr. Hayashi wished to distance himself from the slum origins of his late Master's Reiki practice. In fact, Dr. Hayashi's practice had a firm policy of going to wherever Reiki was needed; regardless of where the call came from, no matter how impoverished the sufferer, Reiki would always be given if requested. However, his records showed that the poor and uneducated were more likely to seek healing's tangible symbols (drugs and surgery) for their ailments, whereas the better-educated (who, of course, usually came from the wealthier classes) tended to understand and more readily accept the concept of taking responsibility for their own healing offered by Reiki. Sadly his own experiences had confirmed those of Dr. Usui's before him.

So far, the story of Reiki has had an almost exclusively Japanese setting. Now, into this quiet, traditional, even inward-looking atmosphere, there bursts a vital and almost radical energy in the diminutive person of Hawayo Takata, of Japanese descent, but nevertheless a Westerner and a woman.

As a frail child growing up in what is now the U.S. state of Hawaii, she knew hardship and poverty. She worked physically hard and seized every opportunity to overcome the limitations of her background. Her marriage to a wise and sensitive man went some way towards awakening her dormant spirituality but did not prepare her for the trauma of early widowhood. Struggling to survive in the Depression years, Mrs. Takata soon suffered a physical breakdown, and major surgery was advised as the only cure. A further family tragedy led her to visit her parents in Japan, and it was in Tokyo, as she was about to undergo surgery for an abdominal tumour, that she recognised a strong leading to seek alternative therapy. Almost immediately she found herself receiving Reiki from the practitioners at Dr. Chujiro Hayashi's clinic.

Mrs. Takata's insatiable curiosity and characteristic persistence broke down the barriers of Japanese reluctance to share this energy with Westerners and enabled her to learn more about Reiki. After a year of devoted daily practice of Reiki in the home of Dr Hayashi and his wife, Mrs. Takata returned to Hawaii not only healed of her critical medical condition, but with Reiki in her hands and a commitment to apply Reiki to all aspects of her life.

During a visit Dr. Hayashi made to Hawaii in 1938, the Grand Master was further convinced of Mrs. Takata's lifelong commitment to using Reiki. The still young and now beautifully healthy woman was initiated as a Reiki Master and was thus enabled to pass on the Reiki knowledge to others in the West. Encouraged by Dr. Hayashi, Mrs. Takata began to study basic anatomy and broaden her education in many practical areas of healing.

In 1941 Japan's entry into the world's bloodbath was imminent. Dr. Hayashi sensed this keenly and with all the serenity of a Japanese Master he prepared to make what he called his 'transition'. Even though a premonition of Dr. Hayashi's death had called Mrs. Takata back to Tokyo, she did not at first understand what her teacher could mean, because at sixty-two years of age his health was perfect. Although retired from the navy, Dr. Hayashi explained, he could still be called upon to kill in the service of the Emperor. A Reiki Grand Master could not contemplate such action and he had chosen instead to die peacefully at home. After deep consideration, he had decided to confer on Mrs. Takata the role of Reiki Grand Master. As Mrs. Takata shared with his family and the other Reiki Masters the experience of Dr. Hayashi's natural and tranquil 'transition', her way became clear to her. She returned to Hawaii, determined that the gift of Reiki should never again be lost to humanity. She was just forty.

It would be a mammoth task to relate the Reiki adventures and rapidly expanding insights of this seemingly tireless woman during the next forty years of her life. Everything written by her and about her brims over with compassionate energy and a readiness to grow from her 'mistakes'. She gave the impression of being an extremely practical woman about whose person there hung no trace of the guru.

She was a born teacher, and so much of what have become our Reiki guidelines are derived from her experience and wisdom. She always insisted that Reiki be kept simple. Reiki was 'natural' and 'scientific', she said. The Reiki practitioner should refrain from egotistical, complicated attitudes and explanations of what is essentially inexplicable - the 'Universal Life Energy', 'God Power', 'the One Spirit' - which transcends all credibile attempts at definition and is constantly available to all. The Reiki practioner's task is simply to channel this universal healing Energy.

'Keeping it simple' did not, however, rule out the necessity to respect and honour this amazing gift of Grace, and Mrs. Takata had to learn by bitter experience that to offer Reiki where it is not really wanted or appreciated is indeed 'to cast pearls before swine'. Disregarding what Dr. Hayashi had told her about Dr. Usui's experience in the Kyoto slums, as well as Dr. Hayashi's own initial attempts to offer Reiki to the poor and distressed of Tokyo, Mrs. Takata, as an enthusiastic new Reiki Master, began to initiate family and friends in order to encourage more widespread healing. So disbelieving were these people in their own ability to heal through Reiki, that they continued to seek healing from Mrs. Takata, whom they saw as having special powers.

She now recognised her complicity in the undervaluing of the priceless gift of Reiki; this haunted her and she began to insist that, although Reiki was freely available to all who accepted the gift through initiation, a token of commitment should be required from the initiate to ensure that Reiki would continue to be passed on. She felt the Reiki student should be prepared to offer 'a day's wages' for the first degree, 'a week's wages' for the deeper commitment and responsibility of the second-degree initiation and, as an acknowledgment of the life commitment to teach Reiki and to use Reiki to master one's life, Mrs. Takata considered the candidate should be 'prepared to sell one's house'. While the practitioner may offer Reiki freely, the person who seeks Reiki healing should be prepared to 'exchange energy', a practice which safeguards the recipient from an attitude of dependency and the practitioner from the danger of an inflated ego.

Mrs. Takata recognised how readily the human ego can take credit for Reiki's healing power and the survival of Reiki as a respected practice depends upon a reverential understanding of Reiki by responsible practitioners. Those who have accepted initiation have been invested with a great trust which is not only awesome, but always humbling.

Until 1982, Reiki was an oral tradition with no written record of its history and teaching. Mrs. Takata, when 78 years old, recorded an audio tape about the history of Reiki from which the story of Reiki was retold by Susannah Brindle in this chapter. The quality of the tape is extremely poor, but Mrs. Takata's spoken word is very inspirational to everyone interested in Reiki and its true origins. I have therefore decided to transcribe the audio tape word by word and make it into a precious booklet. This will be available through the Reiki Hideaway Retreat.

Chapter 3

The Present Development of Reiki in the Western World

Phyllis Lei Furumoto was the grand-daughter of Mrs. Takata and was introduced into Reiki as a young child. In her late twenties Phyllis commenced travelling with her grandmother in the course of Mrs. Takata's teaching, and in early 1979 she was initiated as a Reiki Master.

Mrs. Takata trained and initiated twenty-two Reiki Masters before her death in December 1980.

On her deathbed she appointed her grand-daughter Phyllis Lei Furumoto to be the successor to the spiritual lineage of the Usui System of Natural Healing.

Phyllis Furumoto, the present Grandmaster of the Usui System of Natural Healing, now lives in the United States of America and devotes her life to promoting the knowledge of Reiki worldwide. She is the embodiment of the traditional principles of Reiki:

> *Just for today*
> *do not worry.*
> *Just for today*
> *do not anger.*
> *Earn your living honestly.*
> *Honour your parents, teachers and elders.*
> *Show gratitude to every living thing.*

In 1983 a group of Reiki Masters, which included the Grandmaster Phyllis Furumoto, founded the Reiki Alliance, which is a worldwide organisation for the support of Reiki Masters. There are about 500 Reiki Masters in the Alliance at present (1993) and they are spread throughout many countries.

An interesting development took place in January 1993. At a Masters' Intensive attended by the Grandmaster Phyllis Furumoto, an important decision was made in which Paul David Mitchell, a Reiki Master from the USA who was initiated by Mrs. Takata, was recognised as the Head of the Discipline. This has been found necessary because of the rapid growth pattern which has led to the need to spread the spiritual demand and workload of the Grandmaster. Phyllis Furumoto continues to fulfil the role of the Grandmaster which came to her through matriarchal lineage of her family and that is something which she can't share. Their intention is that both Phyllis and Paul will bear the responsibilities of carrying the lineage of the Usui System of Natural Healing and they will run many workshops in partnership.

The purposes of the Alliance are:
•to honour Reiki
•to serve as steward of the Usui System of Natural Healing
•to provide community for its Masters.

The Reiki Alliance also encourages a high standard of training and ethics in the teaching of both students and Reiki Masters, and to become a member of the Alliance you have to agree with its guidelines. It is open to Reiki Masters of all background and lineage on the understanding that they acknowledge a commitment to these guidelines.

These guidelines are:
A Master of the Usui System of Natural Healing
• shall be initiated by another Master in the direct lineage
• shall make a life-long commitment with the initiating Master
• shall teach students in the form as laid down by the Usui System

• shall use the teachings of the lineage as a living guide
• shall pay to the initiating Master a fee of US $10,000 (or equivalent in local currency). This represents the quality of commitment. With regard to the actual payment of the commitment, most Masters are prepared to negotiate mutually convenient payment terms over a period of time.

Members meet once a year for the annual world conference and this is a very powerful experience as you meet hundreds of Reiki Masters, who all come from different walks of life, but are all on the same path - the Reiki path. The variety of personalities is tremendous and it is through this diversity that the Alliance shows the huge spectrum and potential of Reiki.

I have belonged to the Reiki Alliance since 1985 and find this network of Masters very appropriate. For me the Alliance is my Reiki Master family. From a practical aspect, if one of my students goes overseas and wants to make contact with Reiki people, it is very likely that I can supply the name and address of a Reiki Master in a certain country. This establishes cooperation between Masters and students worldwide and promotes the growth of community among Reiki people on an international level.

Although formerly a foundation member of the Reiki Alliance, the present Grandmaster Phyllis Furumoto holds no affiliation with any Reiki association, but acknowledges and supports the principal Reiki groups as well as independent Masters. However, the Reiki Alliance recognises Phyllis Furumoto as the lineage carrier of the Usui System of Natural Healing as handed down to her by her grandmother Hawayo Takata. The Reiki Alliance is currently going through an interesting stage in its evolution, and readers who wish to be informed should contact a Master who is a member of the Alliance for the latest developments.

There is another Reiki Master organisation called the American International Reiki Association sometimes known as The Radiance Technique. The A.I.R.A. was founded in 1980 by Barbara Weber Ray and its Masters are spread all over the world as well.

No Reiki Master has to belong to any of these major organisations and so there are also a number of independent Reiki Masters.

As Reiki is the Universal Life Energy and is incapable of subdivision, any apparent grouping is inevitably a recognition of the human factor and its diversity. Always remember there is only one Reiki energy - the energy - as we say, of unconditional love.

Chapter 4

The Principles of Reiki and How to Apply Them in Your Daily Life

The principles of Reiki as established by Dr. Usui (see Chapter 3) more than 100 years ago still have as profound a meaning today as they did then. Consequently, they should always be discussed in some depth by the Reiki Master in the course of the first-degree class, and Reiki students are then recommended to apply these precepts as a basis for conducting their future way of life.

No doubt you, the reader, may have seen some variations in the wording of these Reiki precepts as quoted in different books, or as taught by different Masters. You can put these varied interpretations down to personality, belief system, and the experience of each writer or teacher.

Some people who work with techniques like positive thinking and affirmations would not wish to include the word 'worry' which is normally used in the first precept, because of the word's negative connotation. However, it is important to remember that the precepts should not be recognised as mere affirmations, as they have a far deeper purpose, stemming from the fact that Reiki is a unique wholistic system.

This first precept therefore is intended not simply to deny one's worry, but essentially to acknowledge those worries, to accept them for what they are - the lessons of life itself - and to work your way through them to ultimate resolution. For example, there is nothing to be gained by worrying about the past - for the past has already gone; similarly there is no point showing concern about future events for they may never happen. Therefore it is always best to focus on the present.

The second principle - 'just for today do not anger' - may be approached in a similar way, for the anger should be acknowledged and the cause recognised and addressed, for then it can be allowed to pass on, rather than be retained as unwanted baggage to become an unnecessary burden.

'Earn your living honestly' again has a much deeper meaning than its face value. It is important to lead an honest way of life in your career and in your relationship with others. But it is also recognising the importance of always being honest with yourself, and to acknowledge the connection with your intuition and inner guidance, and ultimately the Higher Self. Without this, you cannot achieve self-respect, self-worth and self-love.

The fourth precept - 'honour your parents, teachers and elders' - has a much more fundamental implication than its literal meaning. It acknowledges the commitment to honour and respect everyone, young and old, for we are all teachers of each other, and at the same time, we are all students through our interaction in daily life. Therefore as we live, so we grow, and learn from and love those with whom we come in contact, for the eternal message of Reiki is that it is the energy of unconditional love.

And so we move to the final precept - 'show gratitude to every living thing'. The acknowledgment of gratitude is a courtesy sadly lacking in modern society; its simple recognition by means of the two words 'thank you' has, alas, become a comparative rarity, especially in modern city life. There are so many things to be thankful for, but, because they are often the simplest things, they receive little or no acknowledgment. Thus, we take for granted the enjoyment of good health, the abundance of our food, the joy of our wildlife and the Australian bush, the beauty of a sunset, the list is endless. So gratitude represents another form of love coupled with respect. Therefore, as we complete each treatment, we always say, **'Thank you for the Reiki'**.

Chapter 5

How to Learn Reiki and Which Reiki Master You Should Choose

People interested in Reiki come from different walks of life. They may have an academic background or they may have little education; they may have been on their own spiritual quest for a long time or they may not have found a direction in life at all. All that does not matter, because Reiki does not differentiate - Reiki treats everyone in the same way. Reiki, being completely positive and being unconditional love energy, does not exclude anyone. No-one is too old or too young to get to know Reiki. No belief system and personal background interferes with the universal life energy, so the good news is that anyone can learn the art of Reiki.

Some have seen the word 'Reiki' and feel attracted by it; some have received a treatment and have experienced the benefits from it with the resultant wish to learn how to channel Reiki themselves. Some have read about it and have made the decision to attend a Reiki seminar. There are also people, who do not know anything about it, yet find themselves suddenly attending a Reiki class consciously not knowing why they are drawn to learn the technique.

It is of no significance what made you decide to learn Reiki. Generally you will be drawn to the Reiki Master appropriate for you. Before making your final choice, I recommend that you ascertain the lineage, background, and knowledge experience of your Master.

By choosing your Reiki Master, Reiki has actually started to work within and for you. Reiki has led you in its direction and Reiki prepared you to take the step to receive the initiation whereby you will become a Reiki channel.

The Initiation into Reiki

The word 'initiation' puts some people off. It frightens them, or the term has a religious connotation. But do you know the real meaning of the word 'initiation'? The original meaning of 'initiation' is in fact 'new beginning' and it comes from the Latin language. Choosing to become a Reiki channel signifies the commencement of another way of being with yourself, with your fellow human beings and with planet earth. This is a vital decision, no matter if you made it on the conscious or subconscious level. The initiation into Reiki is a new beginning and will change your life!

Finetuning and attunement are two words used to describe initiation. In modern terminology, these words may more appropriately describe the initiation process to someone who is not comfortable with the latter term, and they may be easily related to the following example. The reader, when listening to the radio, will be aware that, when tuning into your favourite station, precise adjustment of the set is necessary to obtain a clear, strong signal without interference. Reiki energy is just such a 'signal', and your Reiki Master is the facilitator of that 'tuning-in process', whereby your energy channel is 'finetuned', opened up, cleansed and fully aligned with the energy of the universe.

Your channel is open for the rest of your life and can't be blocked, but if you, however, have the feeling that you have lost it, I encourage you to start treating yourself again and also be open to friends and other people, who may show interest in receiving a treatment. This will reawaken and stimulate the flow of the energy once more.

Students experience the initiation into Reiki in many different ways. Some may have profound sensations, such as seeing colours, feeling white light running through their bodies or sensing the presence of other beings, while others don't have any sensations or the memory of them. Regardless of how the initiation feels to you, if indeed you feel anything at all, it is always certain that the channel within you will be opened once the ancient process of the Reiki initiation is performed. Don't compare your own experience with others, as it may lead to disappointment. The experience of particular sensations during the initiation process is no more than interesting and has no bearing on how well the student will channel the energy. Only regular practice of the art will determine this.

One of my students had what I would call a miraculous happening after she received the initation for the second degree:

As it was a warm, sunny day with a light breeze, I offered to do the initiation outside near a big dam. She sat down, put her very strong glasses under the chair - without them she was absolutely helpless - and closed her eyes, so that I could proceed. After I had finished the initiation I told her to open her eyes and give me a sign when she was ready to go back to the house. I waited at a distance of a couple of metres for her to let me know, and while I was waiting I watched her from the side. I saw her opening her eyelids slowly, then move her head to look around. After about ten minutes I asked her again if she was ready to go back but I still didn't get any reaction. I don't know how long I stood there, but finally she got up and turned to me with a very strange look in her eyes. "Klaudia, after the initation when I opened my eyes, I could see without my glasses and I could not believe what I beheld. I saw every ripple on the dam, I saw dragonflies hovering over the water, I saw the shape and form of the gum leaves and the texture of the barks. I now know that I can see without my glasses."

In about two hours her eyesight went back to what was normal to her and she needed her glasses. It didn't worry her at all as she now knew in her heart, 'When the time is right I will be able to see without glasses'.

Without the precise initiation process which is a vital component of the Usui System of Natural Healing you are unable to channel this specific form of universal life force, even though everyone has the ability to transfer some form of energy. It should be understood that in channelling Reiki you are not using your own personal energy.

Sominetta shares her experience before and after she learned Reiki:

When I was a kid I always had the feeling that I could do something very special with my hands. Especially when touching plants and animals I had a sensation that something, which I now would call energy, was flowing through my entire body and out my hands.

Later as an adult I tried to channel this same energy many times - often with a healing success to the receiver - but with a draining and exhausting feeling for myself. I wanted to give my best, and used part of my own personal energy as well as the universal energy. Therefore I was often left tired after giving a treatment, while the person receiving the treatment had the benefits.

For a long time I thought I didn't need to become a Reiki channel, but as I could not keep up with the requests to give treatments because of my own lack of energy, I decided - very sceptically though - to attend the Reiki first-degree seminar. I was amazed at the change within myself. I am now able to give many treatments a day. I am not exhausted any more, but feel energised and refreshed when channelling energy.

The Reiki First Degree

Anyone can learn to be a Reiki channel and no special intellectual ability, no medical or other knowledge, nor any special belief system, religious or otherwise, is necessary in channelling Reiki energy.

Reiki first degree - also called the first level of Reiki - is essentially a 'hands-on' technique in which the hands of the channel are gently placed in a series of hand positions over certain areas of the body. You will see some of these positions illustrated in this book. These positions cover the front, head, back, legs and feet, and have traditionally been found to be convenient.

Students who are learning the first degree are given ample opportunity to practice the routine of hand positions under the caring supervision of the Reiki Master. These include those for the self-treatment, the full-body treatment given to another person, and the short treatment. Students also get information about causes and effects of diseases and learn about metaphysical reasons for illnesses.

The sharing of information about Reiki, its history, and its application and practice occupy the major part of a first-degree workshop, which is normally completed in a weekend. The student's empowerment as a channel is achieved in the series of four initiations/attunements mentioned previously which are spread over the course of the workshop. These initiations are generally conducted on a one-to-one basis between the Reiki Master and the student, and have the effect of opening the student's channel. The channel then remains open for the rest of the student's life.

The techniques learned in the first-degree workshop are complete in themselves and thousands worldwide have learnt the procedures. Many orthodox health professionals, including medical doctors, nurses, psychologists, masseurs and others, have incorporated Reiki into their range of modalities because of its ability to enhance the techniques that they practice.

After using Reiki first degree in their lives for a time some students feel drawn to work with this energy at a deeper level.

It is a good idea to wait for approximately three months before considering whether to complete Reiki second degree. It takes some time, depending on the person, to 'digest' the energy and often students underestimate the effects Reiki has on the physical, emotional, mental and spiritual levels. Take your own time to grow with Reiki. There is no need to rush into the second degree and if this is approached too soon, you are missing out on the wonderful and powerful experiences which the first degree techniques offer you.

Of course, there is no right or wrong way and only you, the student, will know when you are ready.

There are exceptions to this general advice, of course. When you have someone who is terminally ill, techniques of the second degree can be more powerful and therefore more helpful. This could be an appropriate and sincere reason for attending a second-degree class fairly soon after having done the first degree.

The best indicator, however, is to ask your heart and, in this way, you will know whether the time is right or not to make a further and deeper commitment to Reiki by completing the second degree.

The Reiki Second Degree

In Japanese the second degree (also known as advanced degree or level) is called *Oku Den* and that means, 'the further inner exploration of ourselves'.

This describes exactly what happens when a student decides to attend the second-degree class. It provides an opportunity to become more aware and gain more consciousness at a higher level. On the practical side the student learns three techniques.

•The first technique learned is a method whereby the energy may be greatly amplified.

•The second technique, sometimes called mental or emotional healing, works on a very profound level with the subconscious mind. On this level your inner knowledge, your wisdom and your ability to form and direct the path of your life is tapped. This process may enable the conscious mind to become aware of any information, emotions or thoughts, which may then be consciously acknowledged and processed, sometimes resulting in the release of old habits, addictions, behaviour patterns and unwanted attitudes. This can be a very beneficial experience.

•The third and last technique is the absent or distant healing, and for many students this is the most exciting part of the second degree. You will be able to send Reiki to a person, a group of people or a situation no matter how far away they are by focusing the Reiki energy in their direction, again very much like sending a radio signal. You certainly work beyond the limits of time and distance when you do a Reiki absent treatment. Furthermore, this technique may, in certain situations where the motives are sincere, be used to work with those who may have died recently.

As with the first degree you can use these techniques on yourself as well.

The second degree is usually taught over a weekend, and students have time to practice and to work through their own personal emotions, blocks and barriers under the experienced guidance of the Master. Receiving another initiation, the participant becomes attuned to symbols, which are traditionally passed on from the Reiki Master to the student. These symbols are keys which manifest or unlock the energy which is needed to work with the different techniques of the second degree. In Reiki tradition these symbols are regarded as sacred and confidential; the student is required for this reason to commit them to memory as they are never written down except for the purposes of the training. It is important to note that the second-degree initiation has the effect of empowering the symbols so that they will fulfil their function; without the initiation the symbols do not appear to have any active effect.

The initiation into the second degree provides a much stronger flow of energy; the student gains more access to Reiki as the channel becomes greatly expanded.

The acceptance of the second-degree initiation is an acknowledgment of the need to take responsibility for your own life and for your major decisions, and is a recognition of the commitment to use Reiki with the utmost integrity.

A simple way of summarising the first and second degree is as follows:

When you are initiated as a first-degree channel, it is as if you go out into the sunlight with your sunglasses on. Having received the initiation for the second degree you walk outside in the sun without wearing sunglasses. The light is very strong and bright; it may even hurt a little as you are not used to so much light. It also takes a while to get used to the glare and the brightness. So take your time to fully assimilate and accept the shining Reiki light within.

A Word of Advice :

In the previous sections dealing with the first and second degree training I have explained that these are normally accomplished at workshops each occupying a full weekend. When making your choice of Reiki Master I strongly advise that you do not select a teacher who will complete a class in just one day, as I feel this cannot do justice to the training. Furthermore, in first degree I feel it is appropriate that the initiations are spread out, two on the first day and two on the second day and there should be at least a couple of hours between each initiation on each day. This guarantees that you will be able to assimilate the maximum amount of the Reiki energy. I certainly would not recommend anyone to consider learning first and second degree in one weekend.

Also, if you see Reiki trainings being advertised at very reduced fees, I would suggest you question what you get for your money.

Further Reiki Training
(Reiki Intensive - Practitioner Training)

Through teaching Reiki for over eight years now, I have realised there is a big demand for a deeper understanding of Reiki. Although students have taken the first and second degree, they may want to learn more about Reiki and its uses and applications, or they may want to commit themselves more deeply by becoming a Reiki Master. I have therefore developed over a period of several years a week-long program which I call the Reiki Intensive, which has a common underlying theme; however, the routine is arranged to suit the circumstances of each group, its size, variety, and ambitions, as well as the local environment. The Intensive helps students to clarify their relationship with Reiki, with others and with themselves. Students, who see themselves as Reiki practitioners, can obtain many benefits from it as well, while some students do the Intensive because they just want to spend one week with Reiki people.

I prefer to conduct the Intensive in a natural and secluded environment so that students have the opportunity to explore both themselves and their companions without restrictions and limitations set by the outside world. Reiki is a natural modality and therefore has a lot to do with nature.

My students learn to work with meditation, guided visualisation, Reiki chakra balancing, dreams, the book *A Course in Miracles,* body work, Bachflowers, nature and a number of techniques to integrate Reiki into their daily lives. It is a self-assessment workshop and a further step for those who want to become Reiki Masters.

The Path of Becoming a Reiki Master

A Reiki Master has chosen to acknowledge his or her mastery in Reiki, and each path to this mastery is absolutely unique and differs from person to person. No-one is excluded from becoming a Reiki Master once they have taken the first step which is making the commitment. After making this commitment everything else will fall into place.

There are many ways of being committed to Reiki, and many ways of sharing that commitment with others. The process of becoming a Reiki Master is different for each individual and the time involved depends on each person and their needs.

Here are the experiences of one person on this path, which, as yet, has still to be completed. Cathy, who now lives with her husband Charlie in Christchurch, New Zealand, made her first contact with Reiki at an introductory talk which I gave. The kindness of a friend who loaned them the money for two first-degree fees enabled them both to complete the training with me. She writes:

Both Charlie and I felt sure that we were guided by Reiki to become involved with it. The first initiation gave me a sense of 'coming home'. I had never experienced that, and I knew even before the next initiation that I wanted to be a Reiki Master. I felt as though, when working with people, I no longer had to 'do' things, just simply allow Reiki to go where it was needed. This took an incredible load off my mind and emotional body, and I experienced amazing recoveries from illness in people. It seems that my entire association with Reiki since 1985 has been one of letting go and allowing myself to be guided by Reiki.

It was Reiki, in my journey towards Mastery, that told me having a child was necessary before my initiation into Mastery. I was shown that my commitment to Reiki had been covered by my fears and need for approval. It was on an evening of sharing Reiki that I felt the presence of Mrs. Takata, who told me to give to Reiki. I moved past my human fear of rejection, and allowed Reiki to be my guide. I was shown clearly what I had been doing, and was willing to let Reiki bring Mastery to me if that was meant.

Coming to New Zealand was an action necessary to my

commitment, and it has been here that the power of Reiki in absent healing has been shown to me. Each distant treatment has pictures and a powerful feeling of the Holy Spirit which leads me to prayer. I also feel the presence of Mrs. Takata quite strongly.

My heart tells me that Mastery is my path, and I feel blessed that I have finally realised this. My experiences have been very personal, and I feel this is true of every person's journey with Reiki. It has been a journey of empowerment and healing and, in order for me to truly be a channel and teacher of this, I have had to experience it. Reiki has given me 'ME' and I feel that all healing can ever do is return us to who we are.

Through the Healing Centre in Christchurch where she works, Cathy has come into contact with a Reiki Master, Victoria Sinclair, with whom she has established a strong rapport, and with whom she will accomplish the final stage towards Mastery. As she states clearly, Cathy's path towards Mastery is a unique one taken over many years. The important thing to realise is that it is a step that requires much consideration before its accomplishment.

Being a Reiki Master means not only that you give and receive Reiki regularly, but also it means that you make the commitment to teach Reiki. In due course, once you have made the commitment to become a Reiki Master, you now can call yourself a Master Candidate or Premaster. Having entered this new period on your Reiki path you now expand further your knowledge and appreciation of Reiki so that you may learn the art of teaching.

I would advise you to attend the classes of as many Masters as possible to gain valuable experience. Attending such classes also has the important role of enabling you to select the Master whom you feel will give you the most appropriate training, and with whom you feel you have the closest spiritual relationship. This will be the Master who will likely initiate you into mastership. In fact, initiation as a Reiki Master signifies the release of the past in your life and the commitment of a new phase with yourself, with other people and with the planet earth.

In assuming mastery you have now acknowledged your lifelong commitment to the Universal Life Energy. In this sense your life will be guided and your personality will be given choices that will affect many people directly and indirectly. It is my feeling and experience that you must be willing to let go of any commitment you have now. Mrs. Takata said: "You must be willing to sell your house....." and she meant symbolically that your willingness is very important.

Students grow into mastery. It can't be bought or paid for in a literal sense, although an energy exchange is part of the commitment. However, it is a process of evolving your spirituality with Reiki as a means to an end, with Reiki as a focus.

In order to relate to Reiki as a path and a way of being and living your life, it is important to 'take stock' of your own life. On the path to mastery are questions which you have to consider and answer such as:

How are you serving Reiki at present? Have you organised a Reiki workshop and/or Reiki lectures? If not, would you be interested in doing so? What about regular Reiki meetings? How do you integrate Reiki into your daily life? What do your family and relatives think about your path with Reiki? Is there a special field or area in your life where you would like to introduce and offer Reiki?

As a Reiki Master you are a living example of Reiki. It requires maturity, responsibility and integrity. If you keep this in mind following the principles of Reiki and feel guided by Reiki, you will know if this path and commitment is yours.

Part Two

Reiki
in Practice

Chapter 6

How Does Reiki Work?

Reiki is a 'hands-on' technique in which the energy is transferred by laying on of hands. (Note: there is at least one instance, however, of a person without arms being initiated so as to channel the energy through the soles of his feet !)

The person giving the treatment is called the Reiki channel or Reiki practitioner, and the person receiving the treatment is called friend or partner. Through this terminology I avoid any hierarchy between giver and receiver.

Because Reiki is essentially a 'self-healing' energy, I never describe myself as a healer. I am merely the vehicle through whom the energy is drawn by the partner who thereby achieves his or her own healing process.

It is important to recognise, that although I am the channel it is not my own personal energy being used, and in no way am I being drained. In fact, when I channel Reiki, the energy addresses and satisfies my requirements too, as well as the needs of my partner, so we both benefit. I have no control over this energy flow, so I cannot in any way restrict the transfer, which means I cannot give more Reiki to someone I like and less to someone I dislike!

I imagine the Reiki energy entering through my crown, flowing through my body and out through my hands. I gently place my hands on the partner's body; no rubbing or massage is necessary and it is important to ensure hand pressure is gentle, especially over sensitive areas such as the abdomen and the face. If your partner has the misfortune to have a skin disorder, a burn or an area where pain is intense, or for some reason, doesn't wish to be touched, the hands may be held a centimetre or two above the body. The effect will be the same as with direct body contact.

I don't need any special sense to experience the Reiki energy. For example I have eyes to see, ears to hear, a mouth to taste and a nose to smell. Therefore I use these normal everyday senses to experience the Reiki energy.

Everyone can and will have a different sensation either while giving or while receiving this life force. Some students may experience the Reiki energy in a visual sense through the sensation of color; others may have auditory sensations. The most common sensation is, however, experienced through touch, and can manifest most commonly as gentle warmth, sometimes real heat, sometimes cold; there may also be tingling, throbbing or pulsation in your hands, or feet, or even in the whole body. Such sensations may be experienced both in giving and receiving Reiki. Moreover, in a treatment, the experience of giver and receiver can be totally different; for example, one may experience heat while the other may experience coolness.

Years ago I frequently had strong period pains. As my lower abdomen felt sore and my back was painful too, I asked a friend to give me some Reiki. He placed his hands just above the pubic bone, but after about five minutes I asked him to remove his hands, saying, "I think I prefer a hot water bottle, as your hands are so icy cold and that is very uncomfortable". He started to laugh and said, "My hands are more than warm, feel them". When I touched his hands they were, indeed, extremely hot. So I changed my mind and gave it a second try. Again, in the beginning I experienced a cool sensation, but after a few more minutes I felt my 'iceblock' melting. Finally I had a gentle sensation where my ovaries felt as if they were bathed in warm water.

Whether or not there is the experience of any particular sensation, the energy always flows. Furthermore, regardless of any variation of sensation between each hand, the energy flow through each one is the same.

The Reiki partner does not have to undress for the treatment, as Reiki passes through any material - cloth, leather, plastic, rubber, wood, plaster casts and even metal.

I call Reiki an intelligent energy. Although I use a certain procedure of hand positions I know that Reiki flows to where the problem is and to where it is needed most. Neither the Reiki channel nor the receiver can direct the energy to any specific part of the body; I say that the receiver will direct the energy on a higher conscious level so that it will always address the source of a problem. The energy is available any time, day or night, just like switching on a light.

By tradition, I follow a routine of hand positions over the head and body; these positions cover on the physical level the endocrine gland system, and on the etheric level the seven major chakras on the midline. Furthermore, it should be borne in mind that, where there is pain in a specific area, it is always comforting to place the hands on or over that particular part of the body.

Reiki is not an alternative aspirin which only relieves the symptom; the energy will in fact always address the cause as well as the symptom. Let me give you an example. Maybe you suffer from headaches, so the headaches are the symptom, but the cause might be that you have troubles with your eyesight or - on an emotional level - you may not be happy with your job; or the headaches tell you that you may have digestive problems. So Reiki helps you to recognise just that and do something about it, if you wish. You are therefore encouraged to take responsibility for your way of life.

Finally, always remember, if nothing else, Reiki is wonderful for relaxation! You don't have to have a problem before you need to receive a Reiki treatment. You don't need to have an excuse to be in touch with Reiki every day!

After all, you have your Reiki hands with you all the time, so why not use them!

Chapter 7

The Reiki Self-Treatment

Once a student has been initiated into Reiki, the channel is permanently open, thus allowing the Reiki energy to flow freely through that person. The new initiate is now able to give Reiki to himself or herself, to others, to animals and to plants.

Some students use self-treatment to improve their own health and well-being, to achieve inner peace, or to gain a deep state of relaxation. They might be not interested in treating others. However, very often it happens that your initial intent was only to give Reiki to yourself, but you have changed and now you want to share Reiki with others. Whatever your intention is in the first place, it is perfect, as long as you allow yourself to use and incorporate Reiki into your daily life according to your needs.

The self-treatment plays an important role in your well-being, and therefore it is advisable that you do self-treatments regularly. It is as if you recharge your battery daily. You improve or maintain your physical and emotional health. When you give Reiki to yourself you learn to show love for yourself. For many people this is a unique and overwhelming experience, because we don't acknowledge the importance and impact of nourishing and loving ourselves.

Some students also use the self-treatment to come into contact with their inner wisdom. By giving Reiki to yourself you tap into the deep knowledge of your Higher Self, the part of your being which is whole and holy and intact. There you will find answers to either everyday questions or deep-rooted problems; there you also will receive guidance along your spiritual path.

Above. Self Treatment, first alternative, lying down.

Above. Self Treatment, second alternative; sitting, holding arms and hands up.

Below. Self Treatment, third alternative, sitting, elbows on knees for support.

Below. Self Treatment, second hand position, hands over ears / temples.

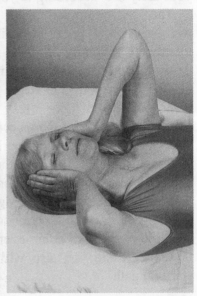

Although there is a set procedure for the self-treatment, you will develop your intuition and find out the best way of giving Reiki to yourself.

You can carry out the self-treatment either sitting in a chair or on a stool, lying on a mattress or in bed.

In the photographs on page 48, I show three alternative hand positions for the first position of the self-treatment; this position covers the eyes, the forehead and the sinus area, and you may select whichever position is the most comfortable depending on the circumstances.

The subsequent hand positions over the ears/temples, and the back of the head, will follow regardless of which of the three positions over the eyes you decide to select. After completing the head positions you will then treat the body positions as shown.

Some basic advice:

Have your fingers together, so that the energy is not scattered, and lay your hands gently on different areas of your body. Make it a nice, comfortable contact and avoid any strain in your arms and hands while you give Reiki. Start with approximately three to five minutes for each hand position and allow yourself to do it longer if you feel you benefit.

In the beginning you may find it very time-consuming to give Reiki to yourself for twenty to thirty minutes. You may even feel it is a waste of your time. This is not so! From my own experience I remember that it was essential to follow the discipline.

Basic hand positions for the self-treatment are shown on the following pages, but keep in mind:
•Start with the suggested routine; but when you are more familiar with it trust your intuition and follow it. Feel guided by your hands and invent your own routines to suit your particular needs. Feel guided by Reiki!

Above. Self Treatment, third hand position, lying.

Below. Self treatment, third hand position, sitting or standing.

Below. Self treatment, fourth hand position, hands on heart centre.

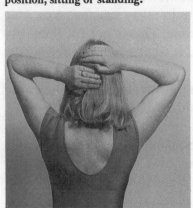

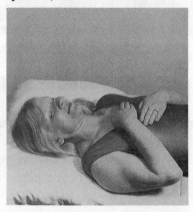

•Do 'casual' hand positions of the self-treatment during the day. For example, you can give Reiki to yourself, when you sit in a bus, when you make a phone call, when you talk to someone, write a letter, or at many other times. Have either one hand or both hands on your solar plexus to be in touch with Reiki all the time.

•When you are in a situation and feel bad vibes, protect yourself by giving Reiki to your solar plexus, either with one hand or with two hands. This hand position works like a protection shield and keeps you safe from those negative energies. You can also use this hand position if you are nervous, excited or upset. If you want to prepare yourself and gather strength - for example you are facing your boss regarding a pay rise - use this hand position before and during the confrontation. The best, however, would be to do a full self treatment or receive some Reiki from a Reiki friend.

•Be aware of times when you consciously don't want to give Reiki to yourself or when you are simply not comfortable putting your hands on yourself. It very often indicates that you refuse - consciously or unconsciously - to be in touch with your self-healing energy. You may have a blockage or show some resistance to working on a personal problem. If this is so, do not stop giving Reiki to yourself; instead become aware of Reiki helping you through this problem and other times of discomfort. Again, another option is to ask a Reiki friend to give you a treatment.

• It is usually hard on your arms, shoulders and hands to give Reiki to your own back. Doing this may merely compound the pain you already have. Your back, on a metaphysical level, represents the support system for the whole body. Having a back problem very often signifies that you don't have enough support and that you have not learned to ask for help, so you deny yourself the need to seek help. After the lack of support in your life has manifested itself in a back problem you need to learn to ask for support; now it is time to ask a Reiki friend to give you Reiki. Don't hesitate, you certainly deserve it.

I personally use a set routine to give myself a treatment. I give myself Reiki for about ten to fifteen minutes in the morning, before I get up. It is worthwhile setting your alarm to sound fifteen minutes earlier, so that you are not hurried in completing the self-treatment. I find the self-treatment brings me into the right mood, and gives me a positive attitude towards things and events that I may be confronted with during the day.

I cover each position with my hands for approximately four minutes or more, and certainly for not less than three minutes so that I do not feel rushed.

At night when I am already in bed I give myself another self-treatment and it happens frequently that I go to sleep during the treatment. When I wake up in the middle of the night, I often find my hands on my heart or my tummy. Reiki flows, no matter if I am awake or asleep. I go back to sleep happily knowing that I am in contact with Reiki and receiving the energy while I am asleep.

The Self-Treatment as a Form of Meditation

I use the Reiki self-treatment as a spiritual practice, for me this is a form of meditation. I have tried many different meditation techniques, but have found none that really suited me. When I became a Reiki channel, I discovered very quickly that Reiki is effortless meditation. I endeavour to empty my mind of thoughts and feelings and, almost automatically, I begin to experience incredible harmony and joy, leading to a deep sense of inner peace. All this happens naturally, without me putting any effort into it.

Those of you who have a particular meditation discipline can easily incorporate Reiki; in fact Reiki enhances any other spiritual practice.

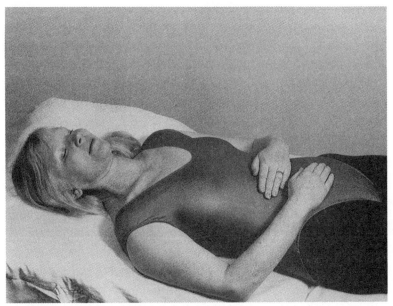

Above. Self treatment, fifth hand position, hands on navel/solar plexus.

Below. Self treatment, sixth hand position, hands on lower abdomen.

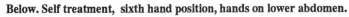

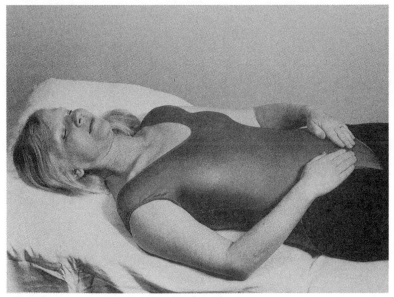

Karmayogini tells her story:

I have practised and taught Yoga for many years and I am also a Reiki channel. Every year I celebrate Guru Poornima, a traditional Indian celebration to give thanks for all gurus past and present who have come to show us the light. The celebration was held at the Satyananda Ashram at Mangrove Mountain near Bega, New South Wales. I shared Reiki with my daughter Alice, and she told me she had an image of an Aboriginal man when she received Reiki from me. I suggested that she ask him if he had a message for her. He told her that he was the traditional owner of the land where we were holding the celebration, and that what we were doing was good. I asked Alice to share this message with the group which she did and again, I felt this experience was an affirmation of Yoga and Reiki and the Aboriginal culture; a perfect example of the unity of all spiritual practices.

Chapter 8

How to Give a Reiki Treatment to Others

There will be a time when you feel ready to offer Reiki to other people. Don't push yourself, if you do not feel interested or confident enough to give Reiki to others just yet. Don't be impatient with yourself and don't judge yourself. There is no 'must' and 'should'. When you are truly ready to share the gift of Reiki and willing to give treatments, the appropriate people and opportunities will arrive naturally.

When your colleagues, friends and relatives know about what you have learned, it is likely they will ask you for a treatment. This is normally a wonderful way of starting to give treatments. It happens only rarely that the people closest to you - for example your husband or wife and your children etc. - are the ones who are extremely sceptical. If this is so, don't force it. Wait until your partner is ready. You have the gift of Reiki in your hands for the rest of your life, so there is no hurry. You also avoid being disappointed yourself.

If you are working in the healing field already, for example as a masseur or naturopath, nurse or doctor, you may find it easier to approach people and offer Reiki treatments. Those who have never done this kind of work before may have some inhibitions to overcome.

Although Reiki is becoming widely known in the Western world, it is still hard to explain in simple terms. In the appendix you will find a short page to write out, if you wish, which gives you a brief, but thoroughly informative introduction to Reiki. Feel free to use this as a guideline, when you explain this ancient art of laying on of hands.

Some people don't want to know on an intellectual level what Reiki is; instead they prefer to experience it rather than talk about it. They are not interested in its origin, and they don't care how it works; they simply feel the benefits from it and, for them, the experience is sufficient.

With children and mentally disabled people you would choose a different approach, as they will not understand the intellectual aspect of a Reiki treatment. It is a good idea to give them an experience of a hands-on treatment and say things like, 'Reiki is like giving a big loving hug to someone'; 'Reiki gives you the love of God' (for religious people) or 'Reiki is like an angel who comes to you and makes you feel much better' (for children). The ways of how you may describe Reiki are endless, but you will find the right way of explaining it if you listen to your heart and speak with love, always keeping in mind that you want to support your friend.

On one occasion a woman in her late seventies asked me about 'the natural modality I practice'. I knew that her husband had been killed by the Japanese during the war, and for obvious reasons she was extremely sensitive to everything which came from Japan; in fact, she hated everything which had the slightest connection with that country. Feeling that she would benefit from Reiki, I explained to her that it is channelling energy through laying on of hands, similar to what Jesus did as described in the Bible. This interpretation was quite acceptable to her, and she enjoyed the series of treatments I gave her.

Following on from the previous general remarks on giving treatments, it is important to choose the right words and the right time to explain Reiki. Your partner, having received an explanation about the way Reiki works can then reach a decision about whether to ask for a healing. It is always important to recognise that it is the privilege and responsibility of your partner to seek the healing rather than for you to force that healing upon him or her. It happens sometimes that people 'love their disease', for it is part of their way of life; indeed, that disease is a crutch in their path through life, and often enables them to gain support from relatives and friends.

To illustrate this very important point I will share with you a case which occurred some years ago in Germany.

I was asked by an elderly lady to give distant Reiki treatments to her; she was suffering from multiple sclerosis and was bedridden. Her son came to her home three times a day to help her with the basic necessities of life, getting dressed, washing, preparing food, even combing her hair. Over a period, there was a general and marked improvement in her condition so that she became very much more independent of the need for her son's help. Consequently it was only necessary for him to come to her once a day. Although I continued giving her distant treatments the improvement was short-lived and she relapsed into a state that was close to her former condition. It was as though she subconsciously realised that her sickness would ensure that she would receive the maximum attention from her son and family.

If your friend wants a treatment just for relaxation and to find out what it is all about, a single treatment will, no doubt, satisfy his or her curiosity quite adequately. Keep in mind that, through Reiki, physical and emotional 'blockages' may be released which may, in turn, result in your friend needing further treatments (see Chapter Nine, 'Growing Pains and Healing Reactions'). So make yourself available for further treatments or, if necessary, refer your partner to another Reiki practitioner.

If people come to you with a certain complaint or disorder, problem or disease, it is appropriate that you start with a series of four treatments, if possible on consecutive days, but certainly as close together as practical for you and your friend. Your friend needs at least the first treatment of the series of four just to relax and to become accustomed to the procedure. Also, the Reiki energy may cause healing reactions, and if your friend goes through these 'growing pains', which sometimes may be a little bit unpleasant, he or she needs to receive follow-up treatments to help through this time of mild discomfort. Never stop giving Reiki treatments when someone is experiencing growing pains. Your friend may become very negative and begin to think that Reiki is making things worse instead of better. Point out that it is a simple cleansing and process of purification and self-healing and that there is nothing wrong or dangerous with the process. The sooner your friend continues receiving treatments, the quicker he or she will feel better.

Four Golden Reiki Rules

These four golden Reiki rules come from my own experience over the years and will give you direction and guidance. From a legal perspective, these rules are very appropriate guidelines in giving a treatment. When giving a friend Reiki for the first time, I emphasise these rules very strongly before I begin with the treatment.

1. Reiki does not replace a medical treatment!

Reiki is a self-healing modality which can be used in addition to orthodox medicine. My ideal would be that the Reiki practitioner, the Reiki friend receiving the treatments and the doctor work together. From my experience it is quite likely that medication could be reduced - often to a minimum - while a series of Reiki treatments are in progress; naturally this, of course, is the decision of the medical or other practitioner involved. It is not our prerogative to replace medication with Reiki.

2. Don't give any diagnosis!

Once you begin giving Reiki to others, you will tune into

your partner's energy field and thus into your own intuition, which will become more and more sensitive with experience. The more Reiki you do the stronger your intuition will probably become. You may feel or sense things in your partner's body or mind, which may lead you to conclusions about your friend's health, state of mind, and general well-being. You may feel very tempted to give a diagnosis.

First, I strongly recommend that you do not give any diagnosis, as - unless you are a doctor or other approved practitioner - you are not allowed to do so. Tuning into your friend's energy field and sensing areas which need more Reiki than others is a fairly common experience. You may become aware that there is currently a lack of energy in a specific area, and it will therefore be your responsibility to channel the Reiki energy into that area by spending more time on a specific position or by covering the adjacent area using extra positions. But remember, it is not your responsibility to diagnose, not only from a legal point of view, but for another very good reason - you do not need to - for Reiki is an intelligent energy and will always address the problem source.

Second, by simply being a channel for the energy you avoid your ego and your own personal thoughts and problems. You don't need to know the nature of your partner's problem, whether it is in the mind, or, if physical, in what part of the body. Through laying on your hands and letting the energy flow, your friend takes as much as is needed for his or her own self-healing process. It seems incredibly simple, but that is all you need to do.

Third, it is important too, that you remember that any suggestion of 'diagnosis' can introduce an unnecessary anxiety or fear in your partner. This is the last thing you desire, as the healing energy of Reiki will enable the negative emotion of fear to be replaced by the positive emotion of love. As the practitioner of Reiki this is your only responsibility - no more than that.

3. Don't give any prognosis!

As you are a channel for the universal life energy, and as the energy is used by your friend for the purpose of self-healing, it is not up to you to say how long it will take to make your friend feel better and how long any healing reaction may last, if , in fact there is one at all. As you cannot know the outcome of the Reiki treatment it is therefore not ethical to give any specific promise of outcome. Of course, you may mention that Reiki is generally a very relaxing and soothing experience, but sometimes problems from the past, which haven't been resolved, may surface. Occasionally people feel the energising benefits of the treatment immediately, but sometimes not, hence it is not appropriate to offer a specific prediction.

When you have given the first four treatments, you should then discuss with your friend the need for any further treatments. You have the option of doing another four in a row, you may choose to do Reiki once a week or maybe when your partner is low in energy or has some sort of emergency. You both come to a mutual agreement as to how frequently a Reiki treatment is required in the future.

The following two cases show how, with Reiki, we can't give a prognosis. Your partner chooses his or her own self-healing process. So it sometimes may lead to a physical recovery of the problem, and sometimes it may lead to a peaceful transition process.

A young woman suffered from breast cancer. She refused to have surgery and didn't want to take any medication. She was full of hatred for the medical doctors and came to me for Reiki treatments. After a series of four treatments she decided to learn Reiki together with her partner. Although she learned Reiki she continued coming for treatments.

The cancer got worse and when she had the next check-up

in hospital the doctors found cancer in her lungs as well. She was very desperate and decided to have chemotherapy. At the same time she asked me to include mental treatments as she wanted to work on a deeper emotional and mental level. The following Reiki treatments were very powerful. She came into touch with important things from her childhood and learned so much about herself, her behaviour patterns and the way she lived her life. She was able to look at a few traumatic experiences from her past and could let go of the pain and hurt which went with them.

After about two months she felt emotional like a new woman and decided to stop having chemotherapy. To the astonishment of the doctors the cancer started to disappear although she stopped the medication. After another few months she was completely clear of the cancer and has been well since, and this is now three years ago. The Reiki helped her to find the cause which led to the symptoms of the cancer. Once she discovered this she made a new choice and the self-healing process could begin.

When B. came to me for Reiki treatments he had had cancer of the liver for about one year, and the doctors had just found secondaries in nearly every organ of his body. They gave him a few more months to live and there was nothing they could do for him except give him high doses of morphine as he was in incredible pain. His quality of life was zero. I saw that he was full of anger and hate because life had apparently treated him so badly. He had bottled up and suppressed all his emotions and seemed to be like a brick wall. Through regular Reiki treatments he started to come into touch with his deep feelings and he began to express his anger, aggression, and his underlying feelings of not being good enough and being a failure. In the next series of treatments he consequently started to recognise his feelings and accept that he was very sick. He finally made peace with his past, with his family and with himself, and died quietly and peacefully while he was asleep. Reiki helped him to let go and to move on.

4. More Reiki is better than less!
A little Reiki is better than none!

The guidelines I am giving you for the full-body treatment, short treatment and self-treatment, are to me the ideal way of treating someone or yourself with Reiki. But they are guidelines and can be changed any time you feel it is important. Reiki will teach you and show you how and when to alternate the suggested procedures. Trust Reiki and feel guided by it!

If you are a beginner and have just completed the first degree, the guidelines help you to remember what to do and how to do it and it may encourage you to use Reiki in whatever way and as frequently as is agreeable. The more you use it in your life, the more confident you will become.

Very often you may be in a position where you want to give Reiki, but you can't set up the ideal atmosphere for a treatment. Keep in mind that you can give Reiki under all circumstances and in all situations and it only needs your willingness to give it.

People can feel the benefits of Reiki even under circumstances which may be far from ideal, such as at health exhibitions and festivals frequently held in Australian cities and towns throughout the year. I attend these regularly with a number of Reiki students and we all give free Reiki treatments. People are very interested in Reiki and will happily stand in a queue to receive a treatment. As we want to give Reiki to as many people as possible, we spend an average time of fifteen minutes on each person, which is even shorter than the 'short treatment' (see Chapter 11). The atmosphere is usually fairly noisy and hectic. Those giving

Reiki often talk and have to answer questions at the same time as they place their hands on someone. Nevertheless, people feel the benefits of Reiki and often report, even after some hours, they still feel the sensations of the practitioner's hands on their body.

Also, by the end of the day we very often treat other practitioners, such as masseurs, Shiatsu practitioners or astrologers. They want Reiki because they are drained by the days work and the modality they practice. As you may already know, Reiki doesn't drain and doesn't make you feel tired, in fact it gives you energy at the same time as you give it to your partner.

Setting up the Right Atmosphere for a Reiki Treatment

Reiki does not depend on setting up a special atmosphere. It flows through you when you put your hands on a person, animal or plant, in fact it even flows when you touch inanimate material. But as we all need and appreciate loving attention and care, you will be doing your Reiki friend a favour if you create a pleasant atmosphere for the treatment. To me it also means that by choosing the right setting, you are showing respect and honour to that person, so that he or she may feel the full benefits of the treatment.

• Make sure that it is as quiet as possible; take the telephone off the hook (and if you have one, switch on your answering machine). Perhaps you can put a notice on the door where you give the treatment reminding family members that you are giving a Reiki treatment. Noise and interruptions don't interfere with Reiki, but both you and your partner will gain more enjoyment from the treatment if there is a quiet and peaceful environment.

• Use soft and gentle meditation music to shut out unpleasant and disturbing background noises (door noises, traffic, loud voices, etc.). If you live in a quiet place the wind in the trees, the singing birds or the crackling of the woodheater will be a suitable background.

• Light some incense or an oil burner. The latter is preferable, as some people are sensitive to the smoke and much stronger aroma of incense. If you have a knowledge of aromatherapy choose an oil which enhances relaxation and cleansing (for example lavender for relaxation and lemon grass for cleansing).

• Set up your massage table, cover it with a blanket or sheet and have both a pillow for the head and also a smaller one for the knees. A blanket to cover your friend - even a light one in summer or a cotton sheet - should be handy, as blood pressure and body temperature may drop during the treatment, or your friend may be sensitive to draughts.

• Wear comfortable clothing and ask your friend to do the same. Depending on gender, your partner may wish to loosen belt and tie, or remove any jewellery, watch or other articles which may be an encumbrance.

• For hygiene, wash your hands and have tissues ready, in case your hands perspire or your partner needs one for nose blowing or wiping tears. If someone is wearing a colorful eye makeup you may wish to cover the face as well, as you want to keep your hands clean. A silk scarf or some similar material is a suitable alternative for this purpose.

• Either remove your own watch or have a clock somewhere in the room so that you can be aware of time, especially if you have another appointment. Tell your partner that the average time for a treatment is approximately one hour and a quarter. You may also suggest closing his or her eyes, and explain that it does not matter if the partner falls asleep.

• Point out that your partner does not have to do anything in particular. Meditation or visualisaton is not necessary. Not doing anything - just being - can be a profound trigger for the self-healing process.

Reiki and Counselling Skills

Reiki does not require counselling skills, but, of course, if you are trained in this area or want to learn them, they are certainly helpful. I can give you a few hints to be aware of, when you have a conversation with your friend.

The most important ingredient, however, is to listen with your heart. I'd like to share a poem with you, which explains in a wonderful way how I'd like you to listen to your Reiki friend. Also, refer to Chapter 23, 'Guidelines for Reiki Practitioners'.

When you listen to me, you affirm me,
but your listening must be real:
sensitive and serious, not looking busily around,
not with a worried or distracted frown,
not preparing what you will say next,
but giving me your full attention and time.
I have ideas to share,
feelings which too often I keep to myself,
deep questions which struggle inside me for answers.
I have hopes, which are not easy to share.
I have pain and fear and guilt I try to stifle.
These are sensitive areas and a real part of me,
but it takes courage to share them.
Please, show interest with your eyes or an occasional word,
attuned to pick up not only the spoken words,
but also the glimmer of a smile,
a look of pain, the hesitation, the struggle,
which may suggest something as yet too deep for words.
Listen! All I asked was that you listen,
not talk or do.
Advice is cheap and I am determined to find out for myself.
I am not helpless, maybe discouraged and faltering,
but not helpless - trust me.

If you take the essence of this poem for your style of talking to your partner, Reiki will do the rest.

Your partner may tell you what I call a 'victim story'. Some people telling such stories may see themselves as victims of circumstances, situations, other people or the world in general. Also, a victim story very often is told more than once, for example: your friend tells you his or her problems before the first Reiki treatment. Next time you hear the same story again, and when the time comes for the third treatment, once more you hear the same story. Your partner is repeating the story over and over again without even realising it. It is not up to you to pass judgment, but you will be helping if you bring it to his or her awareness.

In whatever way you bring it into focus, be supportive and caring. Be detached, but express empathy and sympathy. Let your partner know that you have heard the story before and you have listened carefully with your ears and with your heart as well. Reassure your partner that the time spent with you during the treatment is really his or her time and you are fully supportive. For some this is a unique experience to know that you really **listen**. Don't ask any leading and suggestive questions.

Another option you have is to offer to look at the problem from a different angle. There is always a different point of view to be looked at and your friend is possibly stuck in his or her perception. Bring it to awareness that there is a choice to change the perception of the problem and encourage your friend to take responsibility.

A summary of things to remember:
Don't give a diagnosis.
Don't give a prognosis.
Reiki doesn't replace medical treatment.
More Reiki is better than less.
A little Reiki is better than none.
Point out that healing reactions can occur,

but they don't have to. (Don't state this as a warning).
Reiki is a self-healing energy
and helps you to take responsibility for your life.
Your partner determines the healing, not you.
Point out that you don't use your personal energy.
Enjoy the treatment yourself.

Emergency Reiki / First-Aid Reiki

It goes without saying that if there is an accident or some kind of an emergency, you have to call the ambulance or a doctor. But you certainly should apply Reiki before medical help arrives.

Unless you are familiar with first-aid you should not move the person because of possible internal injuries and fractures.

If the person is lying face-up, put your hands on the solar plexus. The solar plexus is the 'energy pump' and by giving Reiki into this chakra the Reiki energy spreads quickly throughout the body, to settle the person down and reduce any trauma.

If the person is lying face-down, give Reiki to the adrenals, which means your hands are a little bit above the waistline.

If your partner is lying on one side, one hand goes on the solar plexus and one hand goes to the adrenals.

While giving Reiki talk calmly and reassuringly. If you are panicking yourself and upset, do Reiki on your own solar plexus with one hand and give Reiki with the other hand to your friend. You will then both benefit from Reiki at the same time.

Marlene Chignell's story:

Recently I had to be taken to hospital by ambulance. My pulse rate was 225 and my lungs were filling with fluid because of it. Weather conditions were terrible and the first ambulance had to turn back. It took nearly three hours for me to reach casualty. I felt terribly let down that my consistent attempts to use Reiki on myself did not appear to have any effect.

Later I realised that the Reiki had kept me calm for, although I really thought I might die, I was not in the least frightened.

Chapter 9

'Growing Pains' and Healing Reactions

When people come into contact with Reiki, no matter if they receive treatments or if they complete a Reiki workshop, unforeseen things may happen and it is possible that someone may experience 'growing pains', or another term would be a 'healing reaction'. As Reiki cleanses and purifies on the physical, emotional, mental and spiritual level, it can happen that you first have to get rid of your rubbish before you start feeling better. This is a normal process and you need not worry about it. These healing reactions can occur, but they don't have to occur. To expect them would be wrong, and sometimes they are so subtle that you can hardly feel them. It is also reassuring that a healing reaction is never as strong as the original problem.

Growing pains may happen on different levels and they depend on the person receiving the treatment and on the seriousness of the case. They can be experienced in so many ways that I will explain them in more general terms.

Reiki has a normalising effect on all bodily functions. You will find a great change taking place within the body; all internal organs and glands are stimulated to function in a normal manner. Many years of accumulated toxins find their way out through the pores and your perspiration could be a little offensive. Sometimes you may experience skin eruptions. Excretion from the bowel may increase with stools becoming dark and malodorous. The urine flow may increase too, becoming sometimes dark or sometimes light and creamy. You will help this elimination process by drinking plenty of water (eight to ten glasses per day) or using herbal teas. You may be interested to know that tea and coffee do dehydrate your body. So they are not suitable at all.

On the physical level a pain may be experienced; this may initially be quite pronounced, but with time should diminish. Keep in mind that Reiki will lead you to the cause of the problem, the reason behind this physical pain. By acknowledging this, you will allow the healing process to commence.

If you experience the early symptoms of a cold and you receive a Reiki treatment, it is possible you will also experience feverish symptoms. Fever indicates that your body is fighting the complaint, which is a healthy indication that your immune system is coping with the problem. But if you are treating an elderly person or someone with a heart condition, make sure that you deal with your partner in a responsible way. If the fever rises and you are not sure what to do, consult a doctor.

An alternative and natural way of dealing with high fever is the placing of cold compresses mainly on the feet and legs, though possibly on the hands and arms too. The cold compresses draw the heat out of the body and your partner will quickly feel much better.

Emotional and mental symptoms have different manifestations. You may remember a traumatic experience from years past, buried in long-forgotten memories. By recalling it, and coming again in touch with feelings and emotions connected with the event during the Reiki treatment, you get a second chance of healing this traumatic experience from your past. As part of this process you may experience tears, fear, anger, grief, loneliness, or other emotions. It is important that you acknowledge and process these emotions. You should know that the Reiki energy and your practitioner will support you through this process, so remember that, while in touch with the universal life force, you are entirely safe and secure.

Some people feel very tired after receiving a Reiki treatment and this is also a healing reaction. The body tells them they need a rest, so they should listen to its message and allow themselves that rest.

Just the same as crying is a healing reaction, so too is giggling and laughing. These emotions give an enormous relief and sense of release - so don't be afraid - just let it happen and flow.

One fundamental attitude towards healing reactions is that you do not judge them. There are no 'good' or 'bad' growing pains as such, although they might be experienced as 'positive - good' or 'negative - bad'.

When I was a teenager I suffered a lot from sinus problems. I had terrible headaches and a running nose at least once a month. Apart from physically not being well, I felt depressed and was almost unable to continue with my daily duties. The only cure I knew was to take strong medication. The problem became chronic, and when I grew up this sinus problem became part of my life which I had to deal with as best I could. I tried everything, and got used to taking antibiotics when early signs appeared. When I completed my training in Reiki first degree, the following day I experienced all the physical symptoms of a sinus infection. My nose ran, I was coughing and sneezing, and consequently everyone tried to avoid me in case they became infected. To me, however, it felt like a real cleansing, especially as I was very relaxed and happy. There were no signs of a bad mood or depressive state of mind. The symptoms stayed for about a week and then they were gone. Since then I have never experienced any further sinus problems.

In my own teaching I have seen it happening very often that students experience emotional or physical reactions once they have decided to attend a Reiki workshop. Prospective students sometimes ring me a few days before the Reiki seminar takes place and complain about different symptoms, such as headaches, diarrhoea or nausea. Generally they question if they are wise to attend the class because they are not feeling too well. I encourage them to attend the workshop; through completing the training and becoming a Reiki channel their health and well-being improves through experiencing the energy. Healing reactions, which start to happen when someone has made the commitment to learn Reiki - but before they actually attend the class - are an indication of the commencement of the cleansing and purification process.

It is essential to remember that you will not wallow indefinitely in the symptoms of a healing process. So, if you don't feel the best after a Reiki treatment, or after completing the attunement processes in the workshop, remember it is all the more important to keep using and receiving Reiki.

Chapter 10

The Reiki Full-body Treatment

The full-body treatment is normally given with your partner lying outstretched to receive the Reiki treatment. You - the giver - either sit comfortably on a chair or you stand either on the right or on the left side of your partner. The ideal is a massage table, which can be adjusted to your needs as regards height and width of the table. A sturdy dining table or a strong kitchen bench may also be suitable. Especially when you start with Reiki and you don't know how intensively you want to pursue it, you might not be able and willing to spend money on a massage table. A practical and inexpensive alternative is a banana lounge. With this you sit on the floor as it is very low in height, and stretch your legs out underneath. It is also possible to give a treatment with your friend lying on a mattress on the floor, but do ensure that you are comfortable as far as is possible.

If you tend to feel dizzy or light-headed during the treatment or 'spaced out' it is better to sit on a chair with your feet flat on the ground. This helps to improve your circulation and also gives you grounding while channelling the energy. An ergonomic or 'posture' chair is good, as it helps eliminate backstrain.

If you prefer to stand, spread your legs a little bit, especially if the massage table is too low. By spreading your legs you will be able to keep your back straight, thus making the treatment more comfortable for you.

Once your partner is comfortable on the table or mattress and you have covered him or her you are now ready to commence the treatment. Before you start, I would suggest you bear in mind the following points:

• Ask your partner to close his or her eyes.

• Explain that you need a few moments to centre yourself (see section on The Importance of Centering Before the Treatment later in this chapter).

• Tell your partner that you normally don't talk during the treatment, unless something unforeseen comes up, such as:

Your partner starts crying or laughing or shows any other strong emotion and wants to share with you what is happening at the moment.

Some people start chatting the instant you begin with Reiki. Be aware that this can be a sign of being uncomfortable with the silence in the room and/or that your partner doesn't want to recognise specific emotions or thoughts. Reiki will often lead to the cause of the symptom, and so your partner might be frightened or scared to address this and may show resistance. Two gentle ways of dealing with this situation are, first, don't respond or talk, simply listen; finally your partner may become still and allow emotions and feelings to come up. Second, try to find out why your partner started talking the minute you began with the treatment. Be supportive and don't be judgmental.

Your partner shows signs of experiencing strong pain and so you may ask if he or she wants you to move your hands onto another area or if your partner feels he or she can cope with this passing phase of pain or discomfort.

If the pain seems to be unbearable, remove your hands for a while and then go back to the same spot.

The Importance of Centering Before the Treatment

Reiki can be used under all circumstances and starts flowing when you lay your hands on your partner's body. To a certain degree nothing is necessary before you start channelling Reiki. On the other hand it feels good if you centre yourself in your heart chakra before you give Reiki. This process of centering brings you consciously in touch with the Reiki flow, and you may feel the energy running through your body. It also brings you into the appropriate frame of mind. You have various options to achieve a sense of being focused in addition to the centering in your heart chakra. Some of them are:

Say a prayer
Use a mantra
Meditate
Show respect and gratitude to your partner
Be grateful for being a channel
Honour the tradition of Reiki.

Whatever form you choose or in whatever way you combine them, don't use it to attract attention; it should be a silent process. This procedure of centering is a gesture of showing humility, and by laying your hands on your own heart chakra you connect with the power of unconditional love within you, which is simply another way of describing Reiki.

These few moments of quiet in your own space create the process of intent.

How to Treat the Front

Once you have established contact with your partner by the laying on of hands, endeavour not to break the contact, except when your partner is turning over onto his or her front for the back treatment. Your partner may drift away or go to sleep, and therefore may lose his or her sense of reality to some degree. By keeping the physical contact all the time during the treatment you will make your partner feel safe, always having the reassurance of just knowing you are there.

It might be helpful to imagine the energy entering through your crown, flowing through your body and out through your

Above. Full Body Treatment. Front, first position over liver.
Below. Front, third position over navel.

Above. Full Body Treatment. Front, second position over spleen.
Below. Front, fourth position over lower abdomen (V-position).

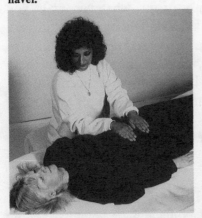 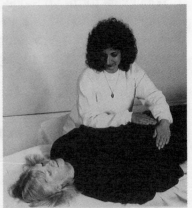

hands. You don't massage and you don't rub, just gently place your hands on the person's body. Use the normal weight of your arms and hands, so there is no need to push the energy in, nor do your hands hover. If you are uncertain, obtain some feedback from your friend and ask if your hands are too light or too heavy. Always keep the fingers together to avoid the scattering of the energy; if your fingers are affected by rheumatism or athritis, just do the best you can.

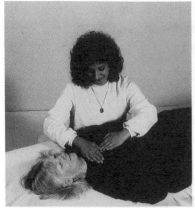 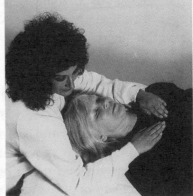

Above. Full Body Treatment. Front, fifth position over thymus and heart centre (T - position).
Below. Head, second position over eyes.

Above. Full Body Treatment. Head, first position over collar bones.
Below. Head, third position over ears/temples.

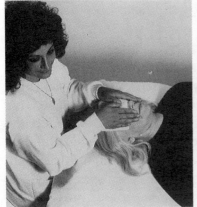 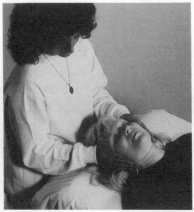

The average time you spend on each hand position is approximately four to five minutes. The more you do Reiki the more you come into contact with your intuition and therefore you will feel guided by Reiki timewise and in what way to use your hands. But in the beginning it is a good idea to follow the procedure of the basic hand positions shown on the following pages.

No matter if you stand or sit on the right or left side of

your friend, the first hand position is the liver. It is your organ for cleansing and detoxification, and by giving Reiki into the liver you begin with a thorough process of purification.

How to Treat the Head

There are students who prefer to start with the head, instead of starting with the front. Apart from the reason of purification, which is previously mentioned, there is one very practical reason why I prefer not to start with the head. At the commencement of a treatment your hands are often cool. The warming up of hands happens for many students during the course of the treatment, and that gives your partner a pleasant sensation. But keep in mind that warm or hot hands don't indicate that there is a lot of energy flowing. You may have cold or cool hands but the energy still flows.

How to Treat the Back

After having done the front and head, it is time to ask your friend to roll over. Stay with your friend, as he or she could be a little 'spaced out' and could feel a bit disorientated. Give your partner a hand, if necessary, to turn over, and cover the partner with a blanket and tuck the arms in. The small pillow goes under the ankles so that the feet are slightly elevated. Some people like a bigger pillow under the chest or pelvis. If possible use a massage table which has a hole provided for the face, as this will be more comfortable for your partner. Use some soft padding around the hole, too.

When you are channelling the energy to the back it does not matter if you start either on the right or on the left side of your partner. Imagine the spine as the midline, where you either put your wrist or your fingertips, and cover the back starting from the shoulders down to the lower back. The importance of certain areas of the back are explained on the following pages.

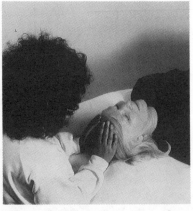

Above. Full Body Treatment. Head, fourth position, back of head.

Above. Full Body Treatment. Head, fifth position over crown of head.

Below. Back, first position over shoulders.

Below. Back, hands over kidneys.

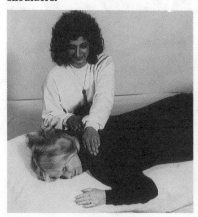

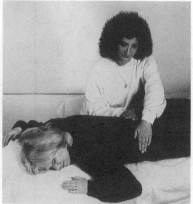

How to Treat Legs and Feet and The Importance of Grounding After the Treatment

The average time you would have spent on your friend should be about one hour. To finish the treatment you will give Reiki to the legs and feet, an important way of ending the full-body treatment. By giving Reiki into the lower parts

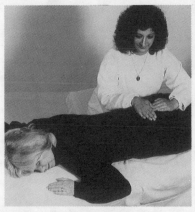

Above. Full Body Treatment. Back, T-position over pelvis/bottom of spine.

Below. Back, hands over back of knees.

Above. Full Body Treatment. Back, hands over soles of feet.

of the body you start a process of grounding. Grounding means that you start to bring your friend back to reality or 'back down to earth'. Your friend has been in a very special space for the last hour, receiving Reiki. Through this gentle, but still very powerful energy, he or she may have been working through many emotions, feelings and problems either on a conscious or subconscious level. Even if your partner simply went to sleep or just experienced a deep state of relaxation, he or she needs an element to reconnect with the daily situation. This grounding process certainly helps to face the normal world.

Apart from the importance of grounding there is another reason for giving Reiki to the legs and feet. If there are problems with circulation in the legs (such as cold feet or varicose veins) you can use extra hand positions, for example the tops of the legs (just below the buttocks) and backs of the knees.

Pay extra attention to the soles of the feet as, by giving Reiki into the soles, you give Reiki to the whole body. Represented on the soles of the feet are all the organs of the body, in what is known as foot reflexology zones.

If you are ever in doubt as to which part of the body to treat hold your partner's feet, and Reiki will do the rest and flow to where it is needed. To me this hand position is both efficient and beneficial.

Chapter 11

The Reiki Short Treatment

The ideal full-body treatment very often can't be done, as you or your friend may not have the time and the space. The situation may not be appropriate to allow you to do a full Reiki. So there is a practical alternative - the short treatment.

It can be given under nearly any circumstances, for example in an office, when you visit a friend and don't have a massage table with you, in a park, in a bus, or before an exam.

For the short treatment, sometimes also called quick treatment, you need a chair where your friend can sit and, of course, your Reiki hands. It doesn't matter what sort of chair you use. It may have a back support (keep in mind that Reiki will pass through any material, so you can place your hand on the outside of the chair-back for the lower positions) alternatively you may use a stool. If a woman is wearing shoes with high heels I would suggest that she removes them. The arms and hands rest on the lap, they should not be crossed. Your partner will achieve a deeper sense of relaxation if the eyes are kept closed during the treatment, especially if there are others present in the room, as he or she is less likely to be self-conscious about receiving a treatment in public.

For the treatment make sure that you have enough space to stand behind and beside your partner. It is of no importance on which side you choose to stand.

I would suggest, however, that you have an extra chair alongside your partner, as it is easier for you to be seated when working on the lower positions of the body, otherwise you will suffer backache through stooping.

Above. Short Treatment, first position, hands on shoulders.

Above. Short Treatment, second position, hands on crown.

Below. Third position, one hand on forehead, the other hand on base of skull.

Below. Fourth position, one hand on the heart centre, the other hand between the shoulderblades.

Because you may be in public, the way you prepare yourself to do the treatment is a matter of personal choice. You may like to explain to your partner and any others in the room that you like to centre yourself by placing your hands for a few moments on your heart chakra, by closing your eyes and going into 'your own space'. To connect with the task and 'switch on the energy', you may even wish to retire - maybe to the bathroom - for a few minutes quiet contemplation. So much will depend on each situation.

I would like to recommend a series of basic hand positions. If you do each hand position for approximately four to five minutes the short treatment takes about half an hour, and this is a good alternative to the full-body treatment.

The procedure for the short treatment is as follows:

• Centre yourself, if appropriate.

• First contact is made by Reiki on the shoulders (you stand behind your partner) - see photo on page 84.

• Both hands go on top of the head; be gentle and don't put any weight on your hands and arms (this hand position can be done either from standing behind or at one side) - page 84.

• One hand on the forehead , the other on the base of the neck - page 84.

• One hand on the heart chakra (chest), the other between the shoulder-blades - page 84.

• One hand on the tummy (navel), the other just above the kidneys - page 86, L.H. photo.

• One hand on the base of the spine, the other hand on the lower abdomen. If your partner is the opposite sex and if you find the front hand position too intrusive then leave that hand on the tummy - page 86, R.H. photo.

• For grounding, rub your friend's shoulders and back and say that the treatment is finished.

You may have noticed that the short treatment covers basically the main chakras: crown chakra and third-eye chakra, heart chakra, solar plexus, hara (chakra of the

Short Treatment, fifth position, one hand on the solar plexus, the other hand above the waistline.

Short Treatment, sixth position, one hand on the lower abdomen, the other hand on the pelvis.

reproductive system) and root chakra. The fifth chakra, which is the throat chakra or communication chakra is not included in the short treatment. If you give Reiki to the throat (one hand would be on the neck, the other one would hover over the throat) some people may get a strangling sensation or some tightness around their neck and throat. As an expression of their discomfort they start to show restlessness and clear their throat. I would normally prefer to leave this hand position out; however if I do use it, I would regard it as an extra hand position, and I would be very alert as to how my friend is feeling.

Keeping in mind that you adapt the Reiki treatment to your partner's needs and to your own, you, of course, can even shorten the short treatment. If someone is open to Reiki but somehow frightened at the same time, a few minutes Reiki on the shoulders may be sufficient to give a taste.

Chapter 12

Reiki and Psychic Skills and 'Can I Pick Up Other People's Stuff?'

Tuning in to your partner's symptoms should not be confused with psychic awareness, for such tuning in represents your sensitivity to a symptom or process affecting the partner you are treating. Psychic skills are not a prerequisite for becoming a successful Reiki channel, but it is not uncommon for some students to experience an awakening or expansion of such abilities through receiving the Reiki initiations or working with Reiki, just as though a veil has been lifted. These skills, once awakened, should be experienced without fear or confusion, and this deepened awareness when used wisely can be a wonderful gift.

Students are often concerned as to whether it is possible to 'pick up other people's stuff'. However, Reiki, being the universal life force that it is, only allows positive energy to come through your channel, while negative energy and 'bad vibes' are dispersed and cannot affect the channeller. Furthermore, the fact that you are not well yourself, or that you are not in your usual peaceful frame of mind, will not affect the transference of the Reiki energy to your partner. However, in fairness to your partner, you will assist better in his or her self-healing process if, when giving a treatment, you have that state of physical well-being and emotional peace that is appropriate to the occasion.

I believe the process of the Reiki initiations protects you from being infected by any disease or emotional problems that may affect your partner. Be aware that it is possible to 'tune in' to such physical symptoms and emotions, with the result that you may experience the same, or similar, sensations as your partner. This can be a common experience for some students. However, this experience does not mean that you take on the receiver's pain or discomfort, for, in fact, those unpleasant sensations should dissipate as soon as the treatment is completed, or soon afterwards. If any such sensation continues to be experienced then you must recognise that - either consciously or subconsciously - you may have chosen to experience that sensation; the blame, therefore, cannot be laid at the door of Reiki.

Sometimes, with the effort of trying to give a better treatment than usual, you may have put your own personal energy into the process; as a result you may appear to have picked up your partner's symptoms. It is essential, therefore, to recognise the difference between your own energy and the energy of Reiki. By examining your motives, you may find that you have allowed your ego to intervene in influencing the outcome in your partner's self-healing process, and then it is important to remember that the Reiki energy will always produce the result that is appropriate for your partner's highest good.

So, always consider whether your personal energy is an intruding factor, and if so, change your approach. But if the unwanted sensations or symptoms persist, it may help to say silently words along these lines, 'I recognise this sensation (name the sensation specifically) is not my sensation. I therefore choose not to experience it and I therefore let it go.' Shaking or flicking one hand at a time (so as not to fully break contact) can sometimes help relieve an unpleasant symptom or pain, for it may be that you are holding or supporting your arms in an uncomfortable or awkward position, resulting in unnecessary tension. You should always recognise any symptom of your own that develops during the treatment. This is an ability that comes with experience, and a problem can arise for the simple reason that you are seated or standing in a manner not conducive to your personal comfort.

Of course, it is also possible that you have developed a symptom of your own during the channelling process. To be able to distinguish between your partner's symptoms and your own comes with time and from experience, but if ever in doubt use the sentence I previously mentioned.

If in some way you have tuned in to your partner's symptoms, always make sure that it is not your province to offer any diagnosis. You may, however, use such experiences in another way for they may guide you to areas requiring more energy, and therefore more time spent working on specific body positions.

Do not jump to the mistaken conclusion that you are a better channel if you experience your partner's pain; this is definitively not true and can be more likely identified as the intrusion of your ego. There is absolutely no justification for believing you have to experience pain to be in tune with your partner; moreover, it is risky to endeavour to attune yourself to the partner's symptom as this can lead to your own discomfiture. You will be thwarted in efforts to be aware of the correct experience; instead, your experience may be a 'phantom' experience.

A number of students also want to learn to attune to the partner's symptom. This can be a risky undertaking for two major reasons. First, if you are not able to tune in naturally then it is important to recognise that you are not ready for the experience. Second, trying too hard can only lead to your own discomfort.

To summarise:

> You cannot be contaminated by anything,
> you are always protected.

You instead may tune into - but do not pick up - your partner's symptoms.

If you have appeared to pick up symptoms, then it was subconsciously your choice at this time.

Remember, don't allow tuning in to lead to a diagnosis.

If you can't attune to a partner's symptom, don't get involved in comparing yourself with those who can. Remember, you are always as good a Reiki channel as any other Reiki person, even if he or she claims to have additional psychic skills. The tuning in is something extra, that's all it is.

Chapter 13

Reiki and: Pregnancy

Reiki is the most wonderful gift which you can give to your baby and yourself, if you are a pregnant woman. Reiki is a powerful tool during pregnancy and labour. Once you - the mother - have been initiated as a Reiki channel, you are able to give energy to yourself and the baby at the same time. You and the unborn baby benefit together.

Be aware of the reactions of the unborn baby both during Reiki initiations and while receiving a Reiki treatment. Reiki can never do any harm, but the response of the baby to the energy can be quite profound and you may be surprised at its reactions. Your baby may kick more than usual or, alternatively, become very quiet and still. Know that your baby is very aware of the Reiki energy and very conscious of what is happening and it may react in ways which you don't expect.

Reiki during labour is a powerful catalyst to the birth process. If you are a Reiki channel yourself, don't stop giving Reiki to your tummy during labour. For some women it is more helpful to give Reiki to their heart chakra, instead of the tummy. It would be of tremendous support if you have another Reiki channel with you. With your own hands you will find it easy to give Reiki to your tummy, while your friend - and this can be your partner or a close girl-friend or any member of the family - is giving Reiki to your back, between the shoulder-blades and lower back in particular. Reiki supports you in an incredible way during labour, and those women who have had children before becoming Reiki channels, and then have subsequently had other children after becoming initiated into Reiki, report big differences in giving birth to their 'Reiki children'.

If you are giving Reiki to a pregnant woman it is essential that you pay attention to a few things.

First, if the woman is in the later stages of her pregnancy her physical comfort on the table has to be considered. It may be helpful to ask her to lie on her side rather than her front or on her back. Her abdomen can be supported with one or two pillows placed underneath her tummy.

Second, because of any reaction of the mother or the unborn baby, be very alert while you give the treatment. If there are any signs of discomfort or unusual movement in the lower abdomen of the mother, move your hands gently to another area and only go back to the same spot if discomfort has settled down. Ask the woman about what to do and what not to do. She knows best where to have the Reiki hands if she trusts Reiki and if she trusts you. To communicate with each other under these circumstances is a big help. Also allow feelings to come up, feelings of pain, joy, bliss, suffering, distress and overwhelmingness.

Reiki and Babies

Babies are souls in little bodies and they have a spirit like anyone else. By now you probably have learned a lot about Reiki, but you might still be unsure how to treat babies.

Because they have a much smaller body you will cover much more with certain basic hand positions. Starting with the liver is still a good thing to do, but because of the size of your hands and the size of the little body being treated you will cover a bigger area, which may include the spleen and part of the intestines. When it is a very young baby and you are simply holding it, be aware that just by touching it you are giving Reiki. Extra hand positions would not be necessary. Babies also love to have their feet done. To do this hold their feet firmly, make sure that it doesn't feel ticklish. Another helpful hand position can be one hand on the little tummy and the other hand covering the upper part of the back. This is a natural way of holding the baby anyway and it is comforting in situations of distress, such as colic. While your baby is asleep you can gently put one hand on the tummy, with the other hand, perhaps, hovering over the head.

As babies grow, they may not be inclined to lie still to receive Reiki. They certainly love Reiki, but to perform it in the way that would be practised on adults, is very often not possible. Be creative! For example:

• While you read a story to them and they sit on your lap, put one hand around their shoulders.

• When they are already in bed, put one or two hands on their tummy and talk to them calmly.

• When they are lying down, one hand goes on their forehead, which is very soothing.

• Keep in mind that you can give Reiki with both hands to different children. One may sit on your right knee, the other on your left. 'Cuddle' them with your Reiki hands and they will receive the energy.

Children are very clear if they want and need Reiki or not. They may have injured themselves while playing - for example they may likely be bruised - and come to you for Reiki. Place the hands where the pain is and don't worry about any preparations. Your child will feel comforted straight away and secondly will use the Reiki energy for self-healing. Very often in a matter of minutes they will jump up and start playing again. Intuitively, they know best, even though you may think this Reiki treatment was not long enough. Trust Reiki by trusting them.

Reiki and Elderly People

For older people Reiki can be the most touching and overwhelming experience. Reiki is a distinctive alternative modality, as there is nothing simpler that you can offer than to put your hands on an aged friend's body. The very nature of Reiki, which involves no rubbing, no manipulation, no pushing, and no pressure, makes the technique with its delicate and peaceful contact the only form of treatment that perhaps will be acceptable, even with the most fragile constitution and physique.

It is also advantageous that it is not necessary to undress, since Reiki passes through clothing, and your elderly friend could feel embarrassed at the prospect of disrobing.

Your friend may suffer from degenerative diseases such as arthritis, rheumatism, stiff joints or backache. Perhaps he or she can't lie down in comfort; maybe your friend cannot lie face down at all because the back muscles can't stretch without involving some pain. It doesn't matter as you still can give Reiki. You have to adapt the procedure of the treatment to what your friend is ready to accept and to enjoy. Different options are:

• Treat only the front, while your friend lies on the back. Support back and legs with pillows, if necessary.

• Communicate to ensure that your friend is pleasantly relaxed and enjoying the treatment.

• Offer the short treatment, so that your friend doesn't have to lie down.

• If your friend is confined to bed, it can be sufficient to hold your friend's hands or feet. Sometimes one hand on the forehead is very soothing and may help to cheer your friend up. Placing your hands on your friend's solar plexus is a good position, too.

• Reiki doesn't need any words, so it might be appropriate not to talk, nor to offer an explanation, but simply to be there surrounding your friend with your loving presence and letting the Reiki flow through you to him or her.

Reiki and Coping with a Life-Threatening Illness

With Reiki you never know the actual outcome of the

treatment. As Reiki is a self-healing energy it is up to your partner - and only to your partner - how he or she uses the energy. In case of a life-threatening illness, such as cancer or AIDS, Reiki, however, can help to improve the quality of life. If you suffer from a serious life-threatening problem I strongly recommend that you either become a Reiki channel or that you receive regular treatments. No matter how sick you are you can become a Reiki channel and this is important to know. If you are confined to bed or for any other reasons are unable to attend a Reiki workshop, don't hesitate to ask a Reiki Master of your choice to teach you Reiki in a one-to-one seminar. Alternatively it is also a good idea to have your family and/or other people who take care of you involved. Maybe you wish to learn Reiki in a cosy and comfortable family situation. This experience will give something very beautiful and special to you all, and members of your family can support you with Reiki. You in return may also feel drawn to contribute and give them Reiki. You are never too sick to give Reiki, and you will not transmit your symptoms to others. By becoming a Reiki channel your energy level will rise in general and you may feel an improvement and a sense of well-being and inner peace straight away.

By becoming a Reiki channel you are independent of other practitioners. You can use Reiki wherever you are and whenever you want it. If you are on heavy medication you may have fewer or no side-effects from the drugs you are taking. You may cope with your disease in a better way or you may experience inner peace.

Through Reiki you also may find the reason for being sick. This cause may have been hidden for a long time and Reiki may bring it up. Don't be afraid as Reiki never does any harm. Reiki will gently bring you in touch with this cause and will give you the strength to deal with it. You may choose on a conscious level to let go of your disease, but it is also possible that you choose to let go of your body. Reiki helps you to get clarity into your life and to make a decision about it.

Reiki does not promise you a cure or necessarily prolong your life, but you certainly will experience inner peace and a better quality of life.

A Healing Journey with Leukaemia
by Jane Graham, Deniliquin, NSW

I was accompanying my husband Neil, who is a sheep-classer, as his secretary on a visit to Argentina.

It was while on this strenuous trip, during which we travelled extensively, that my body said, 'STOP'! While staying with close friends, I suddenly found it a great effort to get out of bed, and the lower part of my body became very painful.

My English friend took me to see a local doctor. He spoke only broken English and seemed disinterested in this Australian traveller, but he gave me an X-ray and sent me off with some pretty strong painkillers.

Next day, with me in a wheelchair, we left for Los Angeles, USA, a lengthy trip in cramped conditions. On arrival there, the pain miraculously disappeared, and I was able to again travel extensively with my husband.

On arriving back in Australia two weeks later my back was troubling me again. Although we thought it was a muscular problem, I looked pale, and my family doctor decided to do a blood test. As a result, I was sent to Melbourne to see a specialist, and, following a bone marrow biopsy, I was diagnosed as having chronic Myloid Leukaemia.

For the next five years, I was treated with tablets, and was able to lead an almost normal lifestyle. I also sought a bone marrow transplant but was unable to find a suitable donor. During this time I changed my diet, exercised, and made changes in my lifestyle to induce peace of mind.

In June 1992, my white cell count reached the acute stage, and I was given chemotherapy, which left me with a very frail immune system and complete loss of hair. Without the tremendous support of my family and my local doctor, I would not have had the will to continue living.

Then I heard about Reiki, and decided to attend a first-degree workshop with my wonderful Reiki Master Jim Frew and a small group of trainees. Although I lay down for most of the weekend, I was able to complete the workshop with these wonderful friends, who have since continued to support, love, and give me group treatments on a regular basis. A miracle occurred when, shortly after, my blood count became normal - quite the most exciting thing to happen in my life.

Although I continue to have medical treatment, my extended 'family' of Reiki friends has given me such hope and love with this life-force energy. Now, with the help of the same Reiki Master, I have completed my second-degree training, a further step I was determined to take. Reiki has taken me on a incredible healing journey which has given me so much joy. Who knows where next it will lead me!

Reiki and the Transition Process

In a situation where it is time for your friend to go and leave his or her body, Reiki is a wonderful means of support, comfort and strength. This support will apply to you too, as well as the friend, who is in that process of letting go of the physical body and the material world. Going into transition is smooth for some and hard for others. Of course, it is not as easy as it sounds, as many are afraid of that new beginning in the next world. They don't know what to expect and that's why they are afraid. Being supported by Reiki is a reassurance that they will be capable of dealing with whatever there is in the new world. Reiki makes you certain of this deep wisdom and knowledge within all of us, and is encouraging you to let go and take this step.

Sue Duff's Experience:

I completed Reiki first-degree so I could give my mother Reiki. She had cancer of the liver and I wanted to assist and support her in any way possible.

I gave Mum hours and hours of Reiki and I am very grateful for the time I spent with her in silence and in quiet conversation. She died very peacefully at home surrounded by her family.

Reiki is wonderful for the giver and receiver. I see it as a meditation where I experience a stillness within and a flow of unconditional love.

I would like to see Reiki playing an increasing role in nursing homes and old people's homes, hospitals and hospices. In these places doctors and nurses are certainly doing their best, but often, because of the constraints of the system, compassion and love take second place. Time for talking and listening, time for a smile and a touch and an encouraging word is very often limited. Can you imagine what a vital role Reiki could play under these circumstances? My answer is 'yes', as I see Reiki as an alternative and completely natural way of being with each other, giving energy for self-healing without depending on pills and life-prolonging machines. You only need your hands, using them to channel the universal life energy with motives that can only come from the very bottom of your heart. This is what I call unconditional love.

Chapter 14

Reiki and Plants

Let me get one thing very clear right from the beginning:
Reiki does not replace watering your plants!

However, if you are willing to apply Reiki to your plants in a responsible way you will have amazing results.

Potplants are very receptive to Reiki. You put your hands around the pot and Reiki will flow through any material the container is made of like plastic or ceramics.

If you are transplanting a plant into a larger pot, give Reiki to the root system first, then place it in the pot with extra soil and finally water your plant. You can add some drops of Bachflower Rescue Remedy to the water, as that will help to overcome the shock of replanting.

If your house-plant has an injured stem or leaf, give Reiki to the wounded part and if possible also to the whole root system.

If you are a first-degree channel and have not learned how to do distant treatments you are still able to send energy to your garden. Find a comfortable spot, and either stand, sit on the ground or in a chair. Centre yourself in your heart chakra - check the neighbours aren't watching you - and then direct the Reiki energy towards the entire garden or certain beds by holding the palms of your hands out in front of you. Do the procedure for approximately ten to fifteen minutes over a week and you will be amazed at the result. If there are people watching what you are doing, just hold your palms in a less conspicuous way.

If you are planting seeds or seedlings, pass your hands slowly over them or hold your hands a couple of centimetres above them.

Have you ever heard of hugging a tree? Embrace a tree of

your choice with your hands and arms, lean or press your body slightly against the tree and let Reiki flow. This is a powerful experience of giving and receiving at the same time. You will sense the strong earthy energy, which comes from the tree into you. Likewise Reiki goes first through you and then into the tree. This creates a forceful energy circle between you and the tree and may give you a deep feeling of being connected with Mother Nature.

When you have read this go and hug a tree!

Chapter 15

Reiki and Animals

Animals love Reiki. They are not intellectually oriented as we are and their mind is not involved while receiving Reiki. They don't question the energy - they either like it or they don't. However, in my experience, many animals appear very attracted to the energy of Reiki.

When animals are seriously ill they are very receptive to Reiki. It is as if they surrender to Reiki. You may watch them carefully, for they may turn and twist to let you know where they want the energy most. Go with the flow and trust Reiki. Don't involve intellectual thoughts as to whether a hand position is right or wrong. Giving Reiki to animals feels to me like caressing them.

When you have just attended a Reiki workshop you may notice that your pets respond to you in an unexpected way when you come home from the class. They either jump straight on your lap to 'suck' some energy from you or they are frightened of it and run away. Some animals watch you from a distance as if they see that your aura has changed as a result of the initiations. They are very in tune with energies in general and I am sure they see the change in your energy field and react accordingly. Don't be impatient if they avoid you for a while (that can be hours or days); give them time to adjust to your new energy level just the same as you are doing yourself.

If an animal is sick and can't move, it is easy to give Reiki and apply a few hand positions. If they tend to move out of reach just give Reiki to those parts of the body where the injury or pain is, or to those areas they will allow you to touch. If they don't want to be touched at all because they are too sore, allow your hands to hover over the area or apply emergency Reiki. It is not a good idea to make the animal stay by holding it too tight. It is better to let it go and then come back later. It has to find its own comfort zone, just allow it time.

If the laying on of hands is not possible at all, of course techniques learnt in the second degree are advantageous.

In June 1991 on a cold and stormy night I found a seriously injured female kangaroo. I could not save her as her hindlegs were a real mess and she had to be shot. When she was lying on the ground I saw something sticking out of her pouch which I believed was the branch of a tree. To my absolute amazement when I had a closer look it was the legs of a tiny joey. I carefully got him out of the pouch. He didn't have any fur, except little whiskers and eyelashes and he was so tiny that I could easily cup him in my hands. After a few minutes my surprise was gone and I felt confronted with reality. How do I help this little thing to survive. I didn't know anything about raising kangaroos and immediately felt very desperate. I tried to make a few phone calls to get advice, but because it was a weekend either nobody answered or at best I got an answering machine. So there was nothing I could do.......except give Reiki. So I sat by the fire the whole night holding this little creature in my hands giving Reiki. The first two days I fed him water with honey and Bachflower Rescue Remedy till I got advice from friends who had raised a baby kangaroo.

Nevertheless, although no-one really wanted to discourage me, I strongly felt the thoughts behind their friendly smiles saying, "What do you know about kangaroos.....it is much too little to survive!"

For the following months I fed him every two hours - day and night. I had him wrapped around my tummy so that he was always in contact with my body and therefore the Reiki energy. At night I held him either with one hand or two, and as you can imagine I often didn't get enough sleep.

But the effort was worthwhile. Now he is a strong, young boy and jumps around in the bush and around the house. He does not want to leave us, although he can any time. I believe the only reason for his survival was the constant application of Reiki.

Chapter 16

Reiki and Food

Being in contact with Reiki means there will very likely be an increase in your awareness in many ways, and your attitude to mundane things may change considerably over time. Take food for an example, the attitude you may have to your diet and its effect on your health may change appreciably. As Reiki helps you to develop your intuition and inner wisdom, your instincts may guide you in the choice of food that is good for you and the rejection of that which is bad for you. It is certainly not necessary to become a vegetarian, but from my own experience I know that students often eat less meat than they did before they came into contact with Reiki. They also become more conscious about their intake of processed food, dairy products, white sugar, coffee, tea and alcohol. If you are not happy with your eating habits, Reiki may help you to change them.

When you approach the table to eat your meal, come with pleasant thoughts. Don't eat when you are worried. Eat with moderation, with a feeling of gratitude and recognise the Great Spirit (or call it God or Divine Power or whatever is the appropriate word for you), who makes things grow and blossom and bear fruit.

In practice, I recognise this by giving Reiki to my food as a form of blessing. It is like giving thanks for having enough to eat and showing gratitude to those who prepared the food with love. I don't make it conspicuous. I place my hands either around the plate or bowl or cup - I also do it this way when I am dining out in a restaurant. No-one needs to notice; it is as if I am saying a silent prayer, as it gives me a deep sense of respect and honour towards life.

An Experience of Reiki Master Peter Didaskalu

The fact that Reiki has a cleansing effect on food as well as on any other material, is well-documented, and is acknowledged as part of the Reiki tradition. This became especially important for me on a personal level immediately after the nuclear accident at Chernobyl in Russia in 1986.

Many people in Europe, as well as other parts of the world, became very concerned as to how they could protect themselves from radiation fallout; in particular, they were alarmed at the high radioactive contamination levels in food, and the possible effects upon themselves. I was resident in Germany at this time and naturally was one of those concerned, and so it was a big relief to me when I heard of some Reiki students who had successfully reduced radioactive contamination in milk by treating it with Reiki.

When I heard about this, I started to suggest the practice of treating contaminated food with Reiki, and I remember very vividly one particular class in Hamburg, Germany. This class took place about two years after the Chernobyl accident. Two of the class members were physicists who were really upset by my claims and gave me a hard time because I had suggested that, by giving Reiki to their food, they could reduce contamination levels of any kind, including radiation. In the lunchbreak of the seminar - which was probably the most hectic lunchbreak I have ever experienced in a Reiki class - one of the physicists clearly pointed out to me, "There are laws of the Universe and you cannot change them!"

We finally agreed to conduct an experiment, and so, a few days later, one of these physicists stood on my doorstep with a half-kilo packet of hazelnuts which had been purchased in a supermarket. He had measured the radioactive contamination level contained in the hazelnuts at the research institute where he worked. This was found to be 48 Bequerel, which is a pretty high level.

He had divided the pack into two equal portions, and

asked me to treat one portion with Reiki, which I did by treating each handful of the nuts for four to five minutes at a time. When I had finished, he took both portions back to the institute to re-measure the radiation levels.

About one week later, I received the result of the assessment by the institute in the mail, followed on the same day by a phone call from my physicist friend. The results showed that the nuts which had not been treated with Reiki still had the same radiation level of 48 Bequerel, while - to his amazement, but not to mine - those nuts which I had treated with Reiki now showed a contamination level of only 18 Bequerel. He was absolutely stunned, and was obviously quite shocked and could not understand what had happened.

We had a long talk together during which he constantly said to me, "This is impossible, what have you done to those hazelnuts?" I, of course, had only one answer, " I treated them with Reiki - you witnessed it. That was all that I did." I cannot give any scientific explanation, but I know this is a wonderful example that Reiki works and for me it was, and is, a confirmation of the huge potential of Reiki.

Chapter 17

Reiki and Crystals

Reiki as a natural healing modality does not need other modalities. It is complete in itself.

However, some Reiki channels feel attracted to combine Reiki with crystals and find that an interesting way of practising Reiki is to complement the energy by using crystals at the same time.

Crystals have an energy and vibration of their own. If you want to use a crystal either for energy work in general or specifically combine it with Reiki then choose a crystal which resonates and mixes well with your own energy field. As people have different energy fields, crystals have unique levels of vibration, too. Both vibrations have to match to get a satisfying result.

Choosing a Crystal

If you are selecting a personal crystal, choose it with your intuition and your sensitivity. You may feel drawn to certain colors, shapes or sizes. Trust your feelings and select one. Hold it in your hands for a while and get a sense for the crystal's subtle energy. The crystal may make you feel happy and content. You may have a burning sensation in your hand or a deep coolness. Perhaps you experience some energy waves coming from the crystal. No matter what the sensation is, feel comfortable with the crystal's vibration as it matches your own.

Once you have decided which is 'your' crystal, you may wish to cleanse it and fill it with your personal energy as well as the universal life force.

Cleansing, Purifying and Loading a Crystal

How you do this depends on the size and shape of the crystal. You can hold the crystal in your hand or both hands or alternatively you hover your hands just above the crystal (more suitable for big crystals and crystal caves). Sit quietly for a while and cleanse it to remove the energy of other people.

Once the crystal is purified give Reiki into the crystal to provide universal life energy, then add your own personal energy to it. At the end, if you wish, use affirmations to load it with your thought patterns and feelings.

Crystals used in Groups and Circles

It is a powerful experience when you do the cleansing and process of purification in a group. Each can load his or her own crystal or you can all load one crystal together. A crystal charged by the entire group will have the energetic vibration of all of you and can help to resolve problems for the group. After charging the crystal you may care to place it in the middle of your circle while you are discussing things. The crystal simply can be used as a focus or help to absorb negative emotions which may come up. You might also be interested in using this group crystal as a 'talking stone' as in American Indian culture. The person who holds the crystal is the one empowered to speak and share, to sing or cry or be silent. That person gets the full attention of the circle and is connected with everyone on a deep vibrational level by holding the talking stone loaded by everyone.

Crystals Used for Healing

It is possible for crystal healing to be used in conjunction with Reiki treatments, but crystal healing is another subject and for more information on this I would refer you to the many books available from New Age bookshops.

However, I would like to quote a personal experience where I have used the combination of a crystal and Reiki as an aid in healing and support.

A good friend of mine was very scared of flying but found herself one day in a situation where she had to take a plane to travel to a certain place.

She responded very well to 'hands-on' Reiki treatments and felt quite relaxed before she went on the trip. But there was some anxiety left and I tried to find another way of supporting her. As she likes crystals very much I asked her if she wanted me to load a crystal with Reiki energy and then take the crystal with her, having it in her pocket or somewhere else close to the body. I told her to hold the crystal any time she felt nervous or not at ease.

When she came home a week later, she reported that she was conscious of the Reiki energy when she held the crystal, and this helped her to overcome any fears of flying.

Chapter 18

Group Reiki and the Reiki Chain

A Reiki treatment given by more than one Reiki channel is called a group treatment, and it does not matter if the group consists of two people or many more. There is no limit to the number of hands as long as there is space on the body of the person being treated. It is a powerful experience to feel more than one pair of hands on your body and the experience can be very profound. I remember that, at the end of a first-degree workshop, my students wanted to practise on me for a while and there was a total of seventeen. They all found room on my body to place their hands and it truly was a unique experience to have all these hands on my body and to receive so much Reiki.

During a group treatment the energy is also amplified. For example: if three channels are giving Reiki to a person, this is in fact the equivalent of nine pairs of hands. We say that we square the number of hands, and in this way the energy is compounded. This principle is called the 'synergy principle'. Imagine five people giving you Reiki - but in fact that is really the equivalent of twenty-five - so contemplate the power of seventeen pairs of hands! Wow!

The routine of hand positions, of course, has to be varied from the one-to-one treatment, as each person will work on a different area of the body. To illustrate how the front, the head and the back, legs and feet can be treated I suggest you look at the photos. Keep in mind that these photos are supposed to inspire you. Don't be rigid! Be creative!

The warm, friendly atmosphere amongst Reiki students while they are standing around the massage table giving Reiki provides a good ground for sharing thoughts and

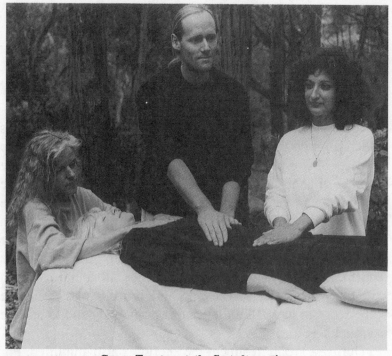

Group Treatment, the first alternative.

feelings, and therefore it is very tempting during a group treatment to talk and chat with each other. Of course, if you talk the energy flow is not disturbed nor interrupted, but the partner on the table may feel differently. By listening consciously or subconsciously to your stories - even if they are related to the treatment or to Reiki in general - the partner is perhaps not fully concentrating and focusing on his or her own self-healing process. The partner may go through emotional or mental healing, which you don't have to be aware of, but by providing silence, he or she will appreciate your full attention and respect and nothing will distract from allowing this self-healing process to happen. It is better to have a break between treatments to have a chat and a cup of tea and a sharing of experiences.

Group treatments in absentia can also be given by using the technique for distant healing. You may gather with a group of second-degree channels and send Reiki to a person, an animal, a plant, a situation or a group of people. If each participating second-degree student is in a different location, but focuses on sending Reiki to a particular subject, the benefits of a group treatment come into action. No matter what the circumstances are for the group treatment, the synergy principle applies and increases the healing tremendously.

Group Reiki treatments may also be used on situations as distinct from human beings. However, to apply group Reiki, whether for local situations or on a global level, I would refer you to Chapter 22 on Reiki Outreach International.

Another technique which you may care to practise is what we call a 'Reiki chain'. In this procedure you all sit on the

Group Treatment, the second alternative.

floor (or on chairs or stand up) and put your hands on the partner sitting in front of you. Give Reiki to the shoulders, back, ribcage or put your hands around the waistline. The partner in front of you does the same to the partner in front. If everyone does this a circle or oval is formed, but this is not essential, and the group treatment could be a long row of people sitting or standing one behind the other.

Participating in the Reiki chain is a very joining and unifying experience and is a wonderful way of either starting or finishing a Reiki get-together.

Chapter 19

Chakra Balancing with Reiki

You will achieve the greatest benefit from a Reiki treatment when you receive a full-body treatment. As it works on the physical, mental, emotional and spiritual level, the full treatment provides the best opportunity for the self-healing process to work, and it also covers the seven major chakras down the midline of the body if the traditional routine of hand positions is followed.

There will be times when you feel that you want to use an alternative to the full-body treatment. This is a modified technique called chakra balancing. This kind of Reiki treatment concentrates on these major chakras - the energy centres of what is referred to as the etheric body - the energy blueprint for the physical body. The term chakra means spinning wheel, as the energy moves in a spiral fashion much like that of a firework, the catherine wheel (see photo/drawing). These chakras are connected on the energy plane with the function of the principal body organs.

For example, the solar plexus is situated in the area of the stomach and digestive system. If there is an emotion which affects you in some way - this can be a feeling of anger, upset or rejection, but it can also be a feeling of excitement and joy - you may have a physical sensation in your tummy, such as a tightness in the stomach, diarrhoea or maybe a feeling of nausea. This is an indication that the solar plexus chakra is out of balance, which manifests on the physical level as the symptoms just mentioned.

As you can see on the drawing, each chakra is situated in close proximity to the body's principal vital organs. So if a particular organ is not functioning normally this will be reflected in a lack of balance in the related chakra which may be too closed, or, in some cases, too open. Therefore you may choose to focus on it by giving Reiki to this particular chakra, knowing that the Reiki energy will restore and harmonise the function of the organ.

Although you may wish to work only on one particular chakra, as there is a problem in this area, I suggest that you start with a full chakra balance, and then spend more time on the chakra that is the site of the problem. Feel free to engage your intuition and inner wisdom as to where you should put your hands.

Preparations for the full-body chakra balance are the same as for the full-body treatment (see Chapter 8). It does not matter if you sit or stand at the right or left side of your partner. After you have centered yourself in your own heart chakra you start with:

• Both hands on the partner's heart chakra to fill it with Reiki.
• One hand on the heart chakra - other hand on the root chakra.
• One hand on the heart chakra - other hand on the hara (sacral chakra).
• One hand on the heart chakra - other hand on the solar plexus.
• One hand on the heart chakra - other hand on the throat chakra.
• One hand on the heart chakra - other hand on the third eye.
• One hand on the heart chakra - other hand on the crown chakra.

The purpose of the constant contact with the heart chakra throughout the course of the treatment is for the following reasons: first, it is the central chakra on the midline, and is also the focal point for the thymus gland which is the key to our immune system. Second, the heart is the centre for unconditional love including self-love, an emotion which unfortunately is sadly lacking today.

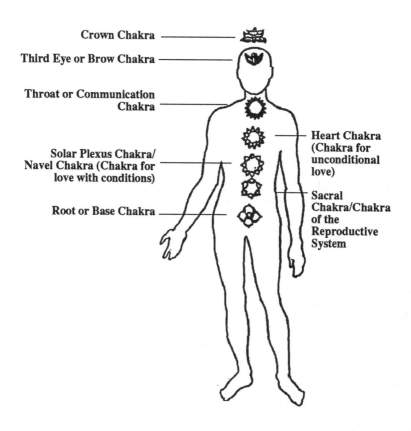

Crown Chakra

Third Eye or Brow Chakra

Throat or Communication Chakra

Solar Plexus Chakra/ Navel Chakra (Chakra for love with conditions)

Root or Base Chakra

Heart Chakra (Chakra for unconditional love)

Sacral Chakra/Chakra of the Reproductive System

With this basic chakra balance you cover all chakras equally and, if you wish, you may now work on a selected chakra. If your partner tells you which chakra to choose, treat it according to his or her request. But also be aware of what your intuition tells you; you may offer to give Reiki to another chakra as well.

You can combine any one of the chakras with another. All chakras are equally important, so if one is out of balance it will affect the energy system as a whole. Trust your inner guidance and you will put your hands where they are needed most.

Chapter 20

Reiki and Other Modalities

Reiki and Orthodox Medicine

Keep in mind that Reiki does not replace an orthodox medical treatment, but it blends in very well with conventional therapies. Apart from enhancing the healing process in general terms, the main benefit from using Reiki in conjunction with a medical treatment is that you may reduce any side effects caused by the medical procedures.

The intake of drugs prescribed by your physician may lead to unwanted side effects, the result of which may prevent you from experiencing a state of complete emotional and physical well-being. Regular Reiki treatments will either eliminate or reduce these side effects, and it often happens that the actual intake of drugs can be reduced as well. For example, in some cases of insulin-dependent diabetes, continuous support through Reiki has led to the need to reduce the daily intake of insulin. Similarly, some people may find their dependence on sleeping pills, tranquillisers and similar medication may be reduced.

If you are about to have surgery you may prepare yourself with a series of Reiki treatments a few days beforehand. It will make you feel relaxed and you will approach your impending surgery with acceptance, peace of mind and a positive attitude to the self-healing process. To speed up this process after the operation, continue with regular treatments. If you don't feel like giving Reiki to yourself, or if you are not a Reiki channel, don't hesitate to ask someone for treatments. Even if you are in hospital, it may be possible for you to receive Reiki without it appearing conspicuous and thereby causing embarrassment either for you or your friend or other people in the same room.

Regarding strong medication, such as chemotherapy, Reiki may help the patient to experience reduced or minimal side effects. I can recall one case in my practice of a young lady who received chemotherapy the night before she came for a Reiki treatment. She felt and looked so well that I would not have been aware that she had so recently been given chemotherapy. Then she told me about the treatment and the fact that she had experienced no nausea, weakness, or other unpleasant side effects. It goes without saying that the doctors were very surprised.

The following is the experience of Ken Andrew of Dromana, Victoria, who was advised in late 1992 that he needed open-heart surgery for a triple bypass and valve replacement. The likely benefit of Reiki was an unknown quantity, so he had no special expectations when support with Reiki was offered by Reiki Master Jim Frew. Several hands-on treatments were given prior to entering hospital, followed by daily distant treatments while in hospital, followed by a further hands-on treatment on returning home. He wrote to Jim some three months later:

"Now that my operation is over, I think it might be opportune to give you my thoughts in relation to the Reiki treatments you so kindly provided.

Firstly, I felt very relaxed and had a positive attitude; this I believe permeated through to my wife Pat and the family. Surprisingly, at no time did I suffer any pain - some discomfort yes - pain no! Could Reiki be this good, or is it modern medicine, or perhaps some of each.

At the after-care stage it seemed I required less attention than others about me; this encouraged me and made me feel I was making good progress.

This progress has continued and has been confirmed by

the doctors; in other words, I have had a 'dream run'. I believe Reiki has played an important part in my splendid recovery, and I hope it can help others as I believe it helped me. Many thanks for your support and help."

Reiki and Alternative Modalities

In Chapter 17 I have mentioned that crystals may be used in conjunction with Reiki; this is only one example of combining Reiki with another modality.

When you are initiated as a Reiki channel, Reiki is available all the time. In practice, that means whenever you touch someone or something there will be a spontaneous transference of energy which continues while contact is maintained. So, if you are a practitioner of a tactile therapy, such as massage or Shiatsu, the moment you start to work on your partner's body with your hands, Reiki will be transferred at the same time. As an alternative way of incorporating Reiki you may wish to use 'Reiki hand positions' and simply allow the energy to flow without manipulating, massaging or rubbing your partner's body, especially if there are areas and spots in your friend which can't be touched because of soreness or intense pain.

Here is a suggestion whereby you may combine Reiki with massage. With your friend lying face down on a couch massage the whole back area, trunk, arms and legs. Then ask your friend to turn over on to his or her back and give Reiki right down the front commencing with the head and finishing with the soles of the feet. This is a very powerful experience.

Naturopaths, homoeopaths, people using Bachflowers, and aromatherapists can readily use Reiki in combination with their chosen modality.

If someone, for example, is prescribed a homoeopathic remedy by myself, I first give Reiki to the bottle containing the remedy, and if the person receiving the remedy is a Reiki channel as well, I encourage the recipient to give Reiki to the remedy each time before taking a dose. To hold the bottle or any other container with the formula with one or both hands is enough to increase the healing energy.

I have also had reports from artist friends who claim improved creativity in their specific spheres after training in Reiki.

The purpose of Reiki is to help to make yourself whole and at one. Reiki does not limit anyone and Reiki does not limit anything, and therefore can and should be applied in all aspects of life.

As a teacher of Reiki, I maintain that Reiki will always show you the path.

Chapter 21

Reiki Network

We have to distinguish between network amongst Reiki Masters and networking amongst Reiki students and practitioners. The first one was briefly mentioned in Chapter Three and I will discuss the network amongst students in this chapter.

For some students there is no need to be actively part of the Reiki community, and therefore they would not be interested in attending Reiki meetings and/or review gatherings. They may use the Reiki only on themselves and don't feel like sharing Reiki with others at all. If you are one of those, enjoy Reiki thoroughly. If you are one of those who wants to be involved in the Reiki community you have several options of doing so:

• Find one or more Reiki channels with whom you share regular Reiki treatments. You will always have your batteries charged and you also can discuss your personal issues - if you want to - which may come up during Reiki treatments. You also maintain your confidence in giving Reiki, and in doing so you will gain further experience.

• Enquire if there are any Reiki meetings in your area, which are either run by a Reiki Master or by a Reiki student. New Age magazines, posters in health-food shops and spiritually oriented bookshops often have information of such gatherings. Also ask the Reiki Master who initiated you. If there are none of these sources to turn to, you may start your own regular Reiki group (see Chapter 23). Regular group and public meetings have the benefit that you get a wide range of Reiki channels together and that means a big variety of experience. You are also able not only to give Reiki, but to receive a treatment yourself. Meetings may also be open to the general public so that those who are unfamiliar can discover more about what it is and what it does. This is a perfect opportunity to bring friends along who are open to a different form of self-healing and are willing to come into contact with this special form of energy.

• Some Reiki students have organised what they call 'the Reiki hotline' or another name would be 'Reiki telephone chain'. It is for Reiki students, who offer their service in case of an emergency. If there is a person in need of immediate Reiki treatments - either hands-on or distant treatments - Reiki students ring around their friends (snowball system) and very soon there could be a number of practitioners giving hands-on treatments or sending distant Reiki. This is not only beneficial for the person receiving the Reiki energy, but increases the fellowship of Reiki in a wonderful way.

• There is a worldwide Reiki association - called Reiki Outreach International - which is open to students, no matter which Master has given the initiation in first and/or second degree, and to Reiki Masters regardless of their lineage and background.

Reiki Master Mary McFadyen who is the founder of this organisation will tell this story in the following chapter.

Chapter 22

Reiki Outreach International

by Reiki Master Mary McFadyen, Founder

A few years ago, as I saw Reiki rapidly spreading all over the planet, I began to realise what an enormous potential existed if somehow we could pool our energy and use it for planetary purposes. Everyone who has experienced Reiki knows its wonderful healing ability for body, mind and spirit. We have felt its sweetness and strength, and we have observed its intelligence and power. We have treasured it for ourselves, and we have gladly given it to our friends and families.

An idea began to stir in me, and a vision began to develop of many thousands of people all sending this wonderful healing energy to world situations, putting light into darkness, balance into chaos, and peace into disharmony. I saw an incredible possibility. Already, many thousands of people had Reiki, and many more were becoming Reiki practitioners every year. The energy and the people were already there, all that was needed was a network which could link the combined Reiki from hundreds or thousands of people, and direct it towards world crises.

Slowly the idea grew, and at a gathering of Reiki Masters I found myself speaking passionately about this world view. As time passed, the realisation gradually dawned that my next step was to bring this vision into reality. What an enormous challenge this was. How to do it? All I had at that time was a typewriter which I used on the dining table. First, it was necessary for us to move into a house where I could set up a fully-equipped office with computer, laser printer, fax, extra phone lines, file cabinets, desks, etc. All this I had to purchase, and I had to learn how to use the computer. Next, if we were really to be international we needed someone in Europe who was willing to establish an office there. Eventually, Reiki Masters Jürgen Dotter and Gerda Drescher volunteered to undertake this huge task.

And what about our name? From the very first formulation of this idea, the name was there: Reiki Outreach International. From the beginning it felt as though R.O.I. existed fully developed in the ether, and that our task was to bring it into physical manifestation, intact and workable. Thus, after much work, planning, and effort, Reiki Outreach International was born on June 20, 1990. A letter of invitation was sent out to 3,000 people in the U.S. and Europe stating the purposes and goals of R.O.I:

• To create a service organisation dedicated to using Reiki on a global scale for our planetary and collective good.

• To establish a worldwide network of communication to make this possible.

• For members to send Reiki as often as possible to specific world crises and events.

• To be open to all Reiki people, regardless of background or lineage.

• To rely on the generosity of members for donations, rather than to make membership of the organisation dependant upon a mandatory fee structure.

• To develop, as circumstances permit, other projects in which members can participate.

The response to our invitation was gratifying. By the end of 1990 Reiki Outreach International had 600 members, and now, in the spring of 1993, we have approaching 1,500 members with our numbers growing every month. The majority of our members at present are in the U.S. and Germany, while Switzerland and Australia also have about 200 members each. Other countries where we have a growing membership are England, Denmark, The Netherlands, Canada, New Zealand, and Brazil and, as the word spreads, Reiki people in many parts of the world join in our efforts. We have members in Hong Kong, Singapore, India, many Central and South American countries, and other European countries.

Thanks to authors Bodo Baginski and Shalila Sharamon, who have provided details of various Reiki organisations in the back of their excellent book *Reiki: Universal Life Energy*, information about R.O.I. is reaching many additional people who are delighted to discover that there is a worldwide Reiki organisation to which they can belong, and through which they can make a contribution to the world community.

When the invitation to join Reiki Outreach International was received by my friend Reiki Master, Klaudia Hochhuth in Australia, she immediately responded by writing to ask how she could help. Klaudia proceeded to establish an R.O.I. office for the Southern Hemisphere in her home in Ballarat, west of Melbourne, Victoria, and she has selflessly served as the Australian Co-ordinator since 1990. In Switzerland, also, an R.O.I. office was established in 1990 by Reiki Master, Regula Linck, who recently handed this function over to Reiki Master Esther Schönbächler von Burg who is now the Swiss Co-ordinator. Other centres and offices are gradually being established as R.O.I. becomes a global organisation with members all over the world.

The immense amount of work required to operate Reiki Outreach International has been done voluntarily until now. The Co-ordinators in particular do a tremendous amount of work as a service to the Reiki community and the planet as a whole. All the necessary equipment needed, such as computers, software, typewriters, fax machines, answering machines, etc. are provided by the Co-ordinators at their own expense. Similarly, the telephone answering machines through which R.O.I. informs members of the situations to which we are currently sending our combined Reiki transmissions, are provided and maintained at their own expense by the splendid and dedicated volunteers who make our network possible. Donations from members are used primarily to cover the heavy costs of postage, telephones/fax machines, and printing.

As we expand, and the workload ever increases, the need for our members and supporters to donate regularly and generously becomes greater, so that essential professional help can be utilised which will allow R.O.I. to continue to do its planetary work on an ever-increasing scale.

Our newsletter keeps members informed of our progress and projects. Our major project at present (other than the transmissions to world situations which are the foundation of R.O.I.), is our Children's Project. For several years I very much wanted to help some of the thousands of AIDS babies and abandoned children in Romanian orphanages, where they live in appalling conditions. After much effort, finally I was able to launch this program through contact with Mary Thompson of Oregon, U.S.A., who spent over a year in Romania helping in an orphanage. With photographs and information provided by Mary, Reiki Outreach International began the Children's Project in December, 1991. Through this program members make a commitment to send Reiki to a specific child daily for three months, and then continue or stop as they wish. Many children have received Reiki from groups of members who take turns to send Reiki to a particular child. The program is extremely successful. Nearly 150 children so far have received extensive Reiki from over 200 members, and many changes have taken place for the children. The volunteers, too, have been profoundly affected by their work with the children, and many have written to say how much they have been touched and rewarded by their connection with a child.

Our collective transmissions to world situations have also

had impact. Although it is impossible to quantify or prove specific results, events themselves often indicate the effect that our Reiki (combined with the prayers and energy of the many people around the globe who may also be focusing on a particular situation) has had in specific circumstances. One such example was the dowsing of the oil fires in Kuwait in 1991. At the time that this crisis developed the existing technology for putting out the fires would have required five years to complete the task. It was accomplished in eight months. On March 29, when Reiki Outreach International began to put Reiki into this situation, 500 fires were burning.When we moved on to another crisis on May 6, ninety of the fires had been extinguished, and the job was completed in only eight months. I have no doubt that Reiki promoted and assisted the inspiration which led the fire-fighters to be able to jerry-rig the ingenious devices with which they put out the fires. Similarly, we were focusing on the drought in Africa as early as July, 1991, many months before it became a major news item. A personal story recently related by one of our members, whose daughter-in-law's family was still in Somalia at that time, again reflected the power and effect of our united efforts.

By sending the combined Reiki of hundreds and thousands of people to specific situations, we are able to promote healing, harmony and peace for our planet and humanity on a scale infinitely vaster than our separate, personal efforts could possibly achieve. If you are not yet a member of Reiki Outreach International, I warmly invite you to join us now in our global vision.

For contact addresses and telephone numbers see the Appendix on page 139.

Chapter 23

Ethical and Practical Guidelines for Reiki Practitioners

The following guidelines are not only appropriate for persons who wish to practice Reiki on a professional basis, but are also a guide for those people who wish to organise their own groups which may or may not be open to the public. These are not rigid guidelines and may need to be varied to suit individual situations and circumstances.

A Reiki practitioner is not a healer or a clairvoyant !

A Reiki practitioner is a Reiki energy channel, who is a facilitator for self-healing.

We regard a person coming for a Reiki treatment not as a patient or a client, but as a friend or partner.

In this way we endeavour to avoid any hierarchy between the giver and the receiver.

A Reiki practitioner has preferably completed the Reiki second-degree level, and is therefore able to offer a wider variety of Reiki treatments:

• Full-body treatment
• Short treatment
• Mental/emotional treatment (which can be also be incorporated into full-body treatment and distant treatment)
• Distant treatment
• Chakra balancing.

The Reiki practitioner offers initially four treatments in a row and decides **together** with the Reiki partner which technique is appropriate at the time. After these four initial treatments the practitioner and partner decide together whether, and how frequently, the treatments will be given in the future.

Reiki can be incorporated into any other alternative or orthodox treatment. A Reiki practitioner is aware of this and may be able to tell the partner whether the Reiki treatment should be accompanied by other therapies.

Golden Rules for Reiki Practitioners:
• No diagnosis
• No prognosis
• Emphasise that Reiki does not replace medical treatment
• More Reiki is better than less, and a little Reiki is better than none.

A Reiki practitioner should be aware that it is essential to point out to the friend who is receiving treatment that, for more serious complaints, it is important to consult and be under the care of a medical doctor or other specialist therapist, always remembering Reiki will support any other chosen modality.

A Reiki practitioner is a mature, responsible and experienced person, who is able to differentiate between his or her own issues and the partner's issues. The Reiki practitioner is able to step aside from a problem, shows empathy and compassion, and should be detached. This detachment allows the receiver of the treatment the space and time for the healing process to take place. The Reiki practitioner's only concern in the course of the treatment is the knowledge that the ultimate outcome will always be what is appropriate for the partner's greatest benefit.

What Is Healing?

All disease and discomfort comes from fear, so therefore healing will involve the release and elimination of fear. Part of the healing process means that the person **giving** the treatment (the practitioner) and the person **receiving** the treatment (the partner) **both** experience a sense of well-being and improvement, where there is a complaint or disorder.

In support of these comments on healing I would like to offer the following quotes from the book *A Course in Miracles*:

No Teacher of God (Reiki Practitioner) should feel disappointed if he has offered healing and it does not appear to have been received. It is not up to him to judge when this gift should be accepted.(Manual for Teachers, page 19.)

Healing is accomplished the instant the sufferer no longer sees any value in pain. Healing must occur in exact proportion to which the valuelessness of sickness is recognised.(Manual for Teachers, page 16.)

A therapist does not heal; he lets healing be. (Textbook, page 161)

Setting Up a Reiki Practice

If you work as a Reiki Practitioner, you are a living example of Reiki. You either work:
• From home
• Together with someone else (naturopath, doctor or other Reiki practitioners) in a practice.
No matter which way you work:
• Be reliable
• Set the time for your appointments generously
• Be clear about the energy exchange with your Reiki partner **before** the treatment (recognition of your time commitment in monetary or other means - see comment on Reiki and money, page 136)
• Have a clean and neat appearance
• Ensure that the room where you give the treatment is clean and comfortable
• Offer four treatments in a row, if these can be arranged.

Starting a Regular Reiki Group

• Find one particular day and select a suitable time (you can't please everyone).

Choose between :

• Starting with a shared meal - it has the advantage that people have a chat before the treatment

• Starting with treatments, followed by light refreshments afterwards.

Decide :

• If you want people to bring food for a shared meal,

• or if you ask for a donation to help cover costs (such as room hire, tea, coffee, biscuits etc.).

• Make sure you have enough massage tables or mattresses set up.

As you are the organiser of these regular meetings, allow yourself to be the leader and prepare yourself for the possibility that both students and non-Reiki people may ask you questions.

Hints for Conversation and Communication with Your Partner

Counselling skills are not required, but they can be helpful. The most important ingredient, when you talk with your partner is the skill of being able to **listen** with your heart.

However, some practical hints:

• Don't ask suggestive questions

• Be non-judgmental

• Let your partner talk first

• Show attention

• Be very careful with advice.

Reiki and Money

A Reiki practitioner never charges for the Reiki, because

this universal life energy is free to everyone. However, it is appropriate that the practitioner can charge a fee as an acknowledgment of the time committed.

Therefore the energy exchange may be recognised by:

• A set fee (money)
• Donation of any kind (money or a gift)
• Non-monetary exchange, such as gifts or labour
• Any other barter your partner has to offer (such as exchange of treatments).

The gift of Reiki is valued much more if your partner gives something back in return. But the golden rule is :

Don't refuse a Reiki treatment if the person can't pay!

Reiki and Advertising

It is important to make yourself known as a Reiki practitioner, but don't give people the impression that through Reiki you have found the remedy to heal the world - don't be a missionary.

Reiki spreads through laying on of hands, through word of mouth, or better, through the touch of your hands.

It is helpful to:

• Make yourself known
• Offer Reiki, whenever appropriate
• Arrange to have a neatly printed information brochure, which includes your name, address and phone number
• Have business cards printed
• Place notices and other printed matter in health-food shops, chemists, practitioner's rooms, New Age bookshops etc.
• Organise practice group meetings for your Reiki friends so they may share Reiki amongst themselves and also introduce it to newcomers.

My concluding advice as someone who has been teaching the traditions and methods of the Usui System of Natural Healing since 1985, is to say to you as the student of Reiki -

Keep Reiki simple and pure!

THANK YOU FOR THE REIKI!

Appendix

My Path to Mastery
by Klaudia Hochhuth

The home environment into which I was born was one in which I could hardly have avoided becoming involved with people, as both my parents are social workers and teachers by profession. As a result, since my early childhood I was often confronted with other people's emotions, feelings and problems.

Through this exposure during my formative years, it was almost inevitable that my university career in Hamburg, Germany should be a major in Psychology and Educational Science, and so I graduated with a Master's Degree in Psychology in 1977.

For reasons I could not define at the time, I was not happy with this achievement. However, after learning a lot about the mind, emotions, feelings, behaviour, and the thought patterns of human nature, I decided to focus more on the physical aspect of human beings, and so went on to study Naturopathy and Homoeopathy.

I thoroughly enjoyed studying these alternative modalities, but although I passed my final exams in 1984, I felt there was still something needed to complete my learning process, and give me fulfilment in life.

Because I am a very persistent person when it comes to seeking satisfaction and purpose in my life, I kept my eyes and ears open.........and Reiki found me. Having an academic background I was extremely sceptical, and looking back I can't recall what made me attend a Reiki workshop, as I had never received a treatment before. I was not particularly interested in going further and completing the second-degree training, but I received the money for the second degree as a present and so I thought 'why not'.

During the initiation in the second-degree class something happened to me which I would describe as a reawakening or reconnecting with my Holy Self. For a few moments I had a sense of oneness with everything and everyone - a unique and overwhelming experience which I will never forget. It changed my whole life and triggered my further spiritual direction. Things seemed to fall into place from then on. I travelled to America and Canada to do further training in Reiki and on St. Valentine's Day 1985 I was initiated as a Reiki Master by Grandmaster Phyllis Lei Furumoto in Denver, Colorado.

I felt guided to start a Reiki Centre in Hamburg together with Reiki Master Peter Didaskalu, and we both taught and practised Reiki full-time.

In 1984 I heard about the book *A Course in Miracles* and was straight away fascinated by its thought system . Together with a German friend, I started to translate *A Course in Miracles* into the German language. It was a tremendous task, but I don't regret one minute of the time spent as I learned so much and it helped me grow, a process that continues to this day.

The path with Reiki is a path of unconditional love and so is the message of *A Course in Miracles*. When I teach Reiki - no matter if it is the first or second degree or if I train a Reiki Master - I want students to experience the path of love and forgiveness, oneness and holiness, care and empathy for each other and for themselves. To me Reiki is the perfect catalyst for that.

I am grateful that I have finally found that 'something' which I had been seeking ever since I commenced my studies. Thank you for the Reiki! Thank you for the guidance which I found in *A Course in Miracles* !

My Path to Mastery
by Jim Frew

I first became aware of the existence of Reiki early in 1988 when a friend told me she had trained in the first degree. I must confess I really had no concept of what the technique was, but I presumably made a suitably polite reply and hoped I didn't sound ignorant. It was only later that year when another two of my friends received treatments from this same person that my curiosity was greatly aroused, as they both claimed that their experiences were quite remarkable. This prompted me to visit the same friend to receive my first treatment, and, although the experience disappointed me in that I didn't enter into a state of enlightened bliss, I was very impressed and curious and felt drawn to learn more. Accordingly, although it involved several months of waiting, I booked to train with Reiki Master Denise Crundall, and in March 1989 I completed first and second degree within several weeks of each other.

Shortly afterwards, I became involved with some active practice groups - the best training ground for learning the potential of Reiki - and I also started working with several cancer patients. I became fascinated with the healing process on the spiritual level that these people received - anger, frustration, and grief for themselves became joy, peace of mind, and a positive outlook - even though physical symptoms didn't always improve a great deal.

I worked regularly with Reiki over many months to gain experience. I reviewed the second degree with Klaudia, the author of this book, in July 1990, and it was as a result of this that I began to set my sights on moving to the teaching role. Furthermore, I had also made the decision to sell my business (a health food shop) so I would have the time to devote to Reiki.

After completing a seven-day Intensive with Klaudia in April 1991, and with a signed contract for the sale of my business, both Klaudia and I felt ready and comfortable about my moving on to Mastership, and so I received the Master's Initiation from her at my home in July 1991.

At the time of writing (March 1993), I have been teaching Reiki for some twenty months. My many students come from varied backgrounds and are drawn to Reiki for various reasons. It is always a joy, however, to initiate them into Reiki, and to watch them grow. Reiki people truly are special people, and you always see changes as they go through their own self-healing processes. I still find cancer patients a special attraction and challenge, because the disease has such a negative concept in society.

There is much responsibility involved in Reiki Mastery, but it is my chosen path and I am prepared to dedicate myself to Reiki as a life-long commitment. I cannot think of a more fulfilling path to tread.

Addresses

The Reiki Alliance
P.O.Box 41
Cataldo ID 83810-1041 USA
Phone: 208-682-3535, Fax: 208-682-4848

A.I.R.A.
American International Reiki Association
(also known as Radiance Technique)
P.O.Box 86038
St. Petersburg FL 33738 USA

Reiki Outreach International Offices,
Worldwide Head Office (Mary McFadyen)
P.O. Box 55008
Santa Clarita, California 91385 USA
Phone: 805-254-4800, Fax: 805-259-1393

> **European Headquarters**
> Postfach 326
> D - 83090 Bad Endorf
> Germany
> Phone & Fax: 8063-9242
> **Southern Hemisphere**
> P.O.Box 445
> Buninyong 3357 Victoria
> Australia
> Phone: 053-413 969, Fax: 053-413 969
> **Switzerland**
> Riegelweidstrasse 8
> CH - 8841 Gross b. Einsiedeln
> Switzerland
> Phone: 55-532 171, Fax: 55-537 672
> **Denmark**
> Ballevej 127 - Gammelby
> 7300 Jelling
> Denmark
> Phone: 75 - 88 1853

U.K. Affiliation
8 Ashmore Road
Cotteridge
Birmingham B 30 2 HA
England U.K.
Phone: 021-433 3212

Reiki Hideaway Retreat (Klaudia Hochhuth)
RSD 975 R
Durham Lead 3352 Victoria Australia
Phone: 053-413 159, Fax: 053-413 969

Mornington Peninsula Reiki Centre (Jim Frew)
10 Messines Road
Bittern 3918 Victoria Australia
Phone & Fax: 059 - 83 9971

Summerdot's Design
PO Box 198, Sebastopol 3356 Victoria Australia
Fax: 053-413 969

References

Bach, Edward: *The Twelve Healers*, 1990, The C.W. Daniel Company Ltd., Saffron Walden, Essex, England. *

Bach, Edward: *Collected Writings of Edward Bach*, 1987, Bach Educational Programme, Hereford, England

Baginski, J. B. and Sharamon S.: *The Chakra-Handbook*, 1991, Lotus Light Publications, USA. *

Baginski, J. B. and Sharamon S., *Reiki - Universal Life Energy*, 1988, Life Rhythm Publications, Mendocino, USA. *

Brown, Fran: *Living Reiki - Takata's Teaching*, 1992, Life Rhythm, Mendocino, USA. *

Chancellor, Philip, M.: *Illustrated Handbook of the Bachflower Remedies*, 1990, The C. W. Daniel Company Ltd. Saffron Walden, Essex, England. *

Dwight C. Byers: *Better Health with Foot Reflexology* (The Original Ingham Method), 1983, Ingham Publishing Inc., Florida, USA.

Foundation for Inner Peace: *A Course in Miracles*, 1975, Foundation for Inner Peace, Tiburon, USA. *

Foundation for Inner Peace: *Psychotherapy: Purpose, Process and Practice*, 1976, Foundation for Inner Peace, Tiburon, USA.

Haberly, Helen J.: *Hawayo Takata's Story*, 1990, Archedigm Publications, Garrett Park, USA.

Harrison, Dr. John: *Love Your Disease*, 1992, Collins Angus & Robertson Publishers Pty Limited, 25-31 Ryde Road, Pymble, NSW 2073, Australia. *

Horan, Paula: *Empowerment Through Reiki*, 1990, American Edition by Lotus Light Publications, USA. *

Howard, Judy and Ramsell, John: *The Original Writings of Edward Bach*, 1990, The C.W. Daniel Company Ltd. Saffron Walden, Essex, England. *

Klinger - Raatz: *Reiki mit Edelsteinen*, 1991, Windpferd Verlag, Aitrang, Germany.

Luebeck, Walter: *Das Reiki Handbuch*, 1990, Windpferd Verlag, Aitrang, Germany.

Mitchell, Paul David: *Handbook for Students*, 1985, revised edition for The Reiki Alliance, Idaho, USA.

Rogers, Carl R.: *Counselling and Psychotherapy*, 1942, Houghton Mifflin Comp., Boston, USA.

Rogers Carl R.: *Client - Centered Therapy*, 1951, Houghton Mifflin Comp., Boston, USA.

Tausch, Reinhard: *Gespraechspsychotherapie*, 1973, Verlag fuer Psychologie, Dr. C. J. Hogrefe, Goettingen, Germany.

White, Judith and Day, Karen: Aromatherapy for Scentual Awareness, 1992, Nacson and Sons Pty. Ltd., P.O.Box 515, Brighton Le Sands, NSW 2216. *

(* **Australian Distributor:** Gemcraft Pty. Ltd., 293 Wattletree Road, Malvern East, 3145, Victoria.)

Reference Videos:

Foundation for Inner Peace: *The Story of A Course in Miracles*, 1987, Foundation for Inner Peace, Tiburon, USA.

Cine - Tech Australia Productions: *Reiki - An Ancient Japanese Art of Wellbeing*, 1992, Cine - Tech Australia Productions, Melbourne, Australia. *

What is Reiki?
(Write this definition out to keep)

Reiki is an ancient art of natural healing rediscovered in Japan over one hundred years ago. What is described as Reiki - the Usui System of Natural Healing - can be defined as follows:

• it is a gentle, but powerful 'hands-on' technique, which brings wholeness to both recipient and giver

• it restores the natural balance in the body

• it provides deep relaxation, thus evoking a sense of peace and well-being

• it works on the emotions, mind and spirit as well as the physical body

• it complements - but does not substitute - the healing properties of all modalities including orthodox medical treatment, natural therapies, massage, psychotherapy etc.

• it can be given in conjunction with any other treatment

• it is not intrusive, since the Reiki energy will pass through clothing, bandages, braces, plaster casts, etc., so that no disrobing is necessary

• it has no connection with any religion, cult, dogma, or special belief system and does not involve hypnosis or massage

• the technique can be used not only on people, but also on animals and plants

• to benefit from Reiki you need only be open and willing to receive the energy. Everyone can learn it.